TITHING

Not for the Church

Njikang C. Mebinaji, Th.D.

Tithing Not for the Church

Published by EMEN Press, a self-publishing company.

Unless otherwise indicated, all Bible quotations are taken from the New International Version (NIV).

ISBN: 978-4-9910517-4-6

DEDICATION

To My Beloved Wife:

Catherine

&

My little angel:

Mebilyn

CONTENTS

ACKNOWLEDGMENTS

I am grateful to God Almighty for the inspiration and revelation that enabled me to publish this book. Without His divine supply and encouragement the realization of this piece of work you're about to read wouldn't have been possible.

1

INTRODUCTION

Ignorance is Costly

In my over thirty years of Christian fellowship, I had grown up listening to sermons on tithing in my local church, and based on those sermons I had always believed that tithing was an obligation for every Christian. As a result, I always made sure I paid my tithes correctly and on time. I was not just tithing on my monthly salary, but on every little increase that came my way. I was doing this because my pastor, quoting Malachi 3:8-10, had always told us that if we did not pay our tithes, God would not answer us in times of trouble and that, in addition, we would come under God's curse. So, in order to avoid the curse of God, and without ever taking the time to investigate the Scripture by myself like did the believers at Berea (in Acts 17:11), I had always believed what I was told; so I always made sure I paid my tithes faithfully to the least dime.

However, deep inside me, I sometimes had this feeling that something wasn't just right somewhere when I noticed that in spite of the fact that I was always faithful in my tithe payments, I was not really convicted in my actions. The proof to this was that I was not always happy inside me every time I paid tithes.

According to one survey, of all those who gave to the church in the United States in 2006, as little as 5% paid tithes, and only 9% of born-again Christians did pay tithes.[1] I couldn't have understood any better

---

[1] David A. Croteau, *You Mean I Don't Have to Tithe? A Deconstruction of Tithing and a Reconstruction of Post-Tithe Giving* (USA: McMaster Divinity College Press, 2010), 2-3

the very poor result of tithe payment reported by this survey if I didn't have this inner struggle experience of tithing. The irony in the survey is that the low tithe payment response rate occurred in a time when Americans were 569% richer than they were during the time of the Great Depression of the 1930s. Worthy to note is that even among denominations that emphasize the tithing practice in the United States, the survey reported that no one member from any of the reported denominations gave up to 10% of their income as tithe.

In the same survey, it was discovered that members from the Assemblies of God Church gave 5% while those from the Southern Baptist Church gave about 3% as tithes. [2] Basing our judgment on the findings of the above survey, the question we all need to ask ourselves is this, "If God commanded the followers of Christ to tithe, how come the latter are now hesitant to do so even though they have been richly blessed by God?" From my personal experience, I believe the reason for the low response to tithe payment is due to the fact that followers of Christ have not been convicted by the Holy Spirit to practice tithing. And this is because tithing was an old covenant law, which has been nailed to the cross at Calvary. Practicing tithing is making the finished work of Christ on the cross null and void. This scenario can only be described as a gross denial and betrayal of Christ's completed mission of FULFILLING the LAW.

To continue, even though inside me I knew tithing by followers of Christ was wrong, I didn't have the Biblical facts to justify my case. To the glory of God, the hour of deliverance came during the course of my doctoral research on tithing when I discovered that believers under the new covenant are not obligated to practice tithing as a doctrine. After having found out the truth about the subject in which I, and millions of Christians out there, have been deceived for years, I became so sad in my spirit and thought that it is important I write this book, which I believe will liberate many who are suffering under the same bondage of trying to fulfil a law, which our Saviour and Lord, Jesus Christ, had already fulfilled for us when he died on the cross and resurrected from the grave.

No One is Immune to Deception

No one is immune to deception. No matter how faithful you may be in your walk with God, if you lack proper knowledge of the Word of God, you'll fall prey to deception. I was deceived for years on account of

---

[2] Croteau, *You Mean I Don't Have to Tithe?* 3

my ignorance. The same is true to anyone. The Bible is explicit about this. God's people perish, the Bible says, not because they lack an offering, tithe, or sacrifice to give to God, a beautiful church building where they can fellowship, a good house to live in, or a beautiful raiment to put on; they perish simply because they lack the knowledge of God's Word.

Tithing is Disobedience, Not Obedience

Paying tithes is not being obedient to God. On the contrary, it is an expression of disobedience toward God; the one who practices tithing is trying to do what has already been done by God's Son, Jesus Christ. The payer of tithes is trying to appease the wrath of God by fulfilling the work of the law, which Christ had already fulfilled on the cross. It is for this reason that this book has been entitled, "*Tithing Not for the Church.*"

In this book, we are going to show you why believers under the new covenant of our Lord and Savior, Jesus Christ, should not pay tithes. We will also show you how tithing was smuggled into the Church and how the church leaders, for the sake of their personal interests, have succeeded in getting church members surrender 10% of their monthly income and personal properties as tithes by manipulating the Word of God.

Definition of Biblical Tithing

The word *tithe* has, for centuries, been often used in most Christian circles to the extent that those who make use of this term believe they know exactly what it actually means. If a survey were to be carried out on issues surrounding the subject of tithing such as its authorized givers, content, purpose, place, timing, beneficiaries, and dispensation, one would be shocked to find a high level of ignorance to be exhibited by adherents of tithing.

The word *tithe* in both Hebrew (*Maasar*) and Greek (*dekato*) simply means "a tenth part of." However, beyond this simple definition lies the biblical meaning. According to the biblical definition, *a tithe* does not merely refer to "a tenth part of *anything*." It refers to a tenth part of a *specific thing*. And that thing is either "an agricultural crop grown in the land of Israel" or "livestock reared in Israel." Thus, the biblical tithe is bounded by well-defined parameters. The Jews, to whom the law of tithing was given, practiced tithing within the established parameters. Any practice of tithing beyond these parameters was seen as breaking the Law of Moses.

In the course of this book, we shall look at these parameters in great detail. What should be noted now is this: the biblical tithe was a law enshrined in the Law of Moses that was given specifically to the nation of Israel under the old covenant for the benefit of that nation. Tithe wasn't ten percent of the Jew's monthly income as practiced today in most church institutions around the world; tithe was ten percent of the Jew's harvested crops or livestock.

Tithing in the Church is a Violation of the Law

In my over twenty-five years in the church, I have not seen any church that practices tithing as instructed in the Law of Moses. This is not to commend tithing in the church as it is an obsolete law with respect to the Church, having been fulfilled by Christ by nailing on the cross. When you ask tithe-collecting churches, "Why do you practice tithing?" they will tell you, "It's in the Bible." By that statement they're referring to the Old Testament Scripture. But the question to ask further is, "If they really want to follow the Law of Moses, why do they not do it as instructed by the prophet Moses?"

For your information, according to the Law of Moses, there were three types of tithe: the Levitical, the Festival, and the Charity Tithes. Why do churches practice only one of them – the Levitical Tithe? Let's consider that Levitical tithing is a divine commandment to the Church. Still, a careful scrutiny would reveal that those churches that practice the Levitical tithing do not observe its regulations as stipulated in the Mosaic Law. According to the Law, a further ten percent was to be separated from the Levitical tithe (known as heave offering) and given to the priest to be eaten in the holy place of the Temple. But this regulation, and more as we will discover later, is not put into effect by tithe-practicing churches.

The fact that churches do not practice tithing as laid down in the old covenant Law of Moses speaks volumes. The leaders of these churches know very well that if they instruct their congregation to tithe as instructed in the Law of Moses, their deception will be exposed. As you read through the pages of this book, you will fully understand what *tithing* in Judaism was all about, and why tithing is not meant for the New Testament Church.

The Law of Tithing, a Poison to the Church

"The entire Church has been inoculated," Bruce Wells laments, "with a dead substance known as The Law."[3] That is the reason why Apostle Paul, in 2 Corinthians 3, referred to the Old Testament as "the ministration of death." The reason Paul said this is because any doctrine that is based on performance, such as tithing, obligates you to fulfill ALL the other components of the Law. And because a tither CANNOT fulfill the entire Law of Moses, this leads to their disqualification and death.

For those who are bent on practicing tithing under the new covenant, the dispensation of grace, which era we find ourselves today, it would be interesting to note what Paul said concerning them. The Apostle to the Gentiles affirmed that those who insist on practicing the Law under the new covenant have simply been blinded by a veil. If Satan can't keep you from finding Jesus, he will keep you from understanding the Gospel truth. And that Gospel truth is that your salvation comes from GRACE ALONE, and <u>not</u> from an observance of the Law.

No wonder the Scripture says in Romans 8:1 that "There is therefore now no condemnation to them which are in Christ Jesus, who walk not after the flesh, but after the Spirit." The word "flesh" here refers to *the Law* (this is confirmed by the context and surrounding verses), not to our sinful behavior, as has often been taught by the Church. So if "the flesh" implies "the law," what the above passage is disclosing to us is that there is no condemnation (literally, separation from God) to those who do not walk after the law (flesh). Going the other way round would mean "there is certainly condemnation to those who walk after the law (flesh). "To be condemned for practicing the Law" means "to be separated from God's grace." And this separation brings guilt in the heart of those who practice tithing. This guilt is a powerful tool that is used by pastors to lure members of their congregation into paying tithes. To use the expression of Paul, anyone who practices tithing is in bondage of the law of tithing. Paul often used the term *bondage* to depict "serving the Law."

The position of this book may sound totally strange to you because you have always been taught to give to your local church ten percent of your income as tithe without having been properly taught what the tithing system, as practiced in old covenant Judaism, was really all about. If the truth should be told, no minister of the gospel can teach a biblically-sound message on why Christians should pay

---

[3] A. Bruce Wells, *The Great Tithing Debate: Condemned If You Do, Condemned If You Don't* (USA: Author House, 2007), xv.

tithes under the new covenant without compromising the Word of God. New Testament scriptural proofs legalizing the practice of tithing in the Church do not exist, Bruce Wells writes. "The loud," Wells continues, "finger-pointing, pseudo-authoritative claims are all based on an old covenant that is no longer in force, and/or a multitude of tired, passed-around clichés, all lacking in scriptural foundation" [4].

Regarding the importation of tithing from its Jewish worship system into the Church, Stedman writes:

> "It will be evident ... that the New Testament doctrine of giving is full and complete, lacking no element essential to a well-rounded instruction. There is thereby afforded no excuse for borrowing any features whatsoever from the legal system presented in the Old Testament. To do so is to that extent, to 'fall from grace' to the infinitely lower level of duty and legal obligation." [5]

Grace is the Answer

Grace is the answer to every human problem, not the Law. In case you find yourself on the side of the Law, you may be on the wrong side of God's plan for salvation in this present dispensation. Have you ever wondered why God's throne is identified as "the throne of grace," and not "the throne of the Law?" I leave that to you as food for thought.

Sound Doctrine Is Based On Truth, Not Poetry

I have heard some preachers, in their attempt to manipulate the congregation to surrender ten percent of their income at their feet, utter manipulative statements like, "If you do not pay your tithes, things will be tight for you." And most of the gullible Christians, being carried away by the poetic beauty of such a statement, and for fear of attracting the curse of God, would dash towards the altar to give or pledge a tenth of their possessions. This is the unfortunate scenario that is going on in most churches today. Sound doctrine is not determined by the structural or grammatical beauty of a minister's speech; sound doctrine is determined by the biblical soundness of the message preached.

---

[4] Wells, *The Great Tithing Debate*, 14.
[5] Denis O. Wretlind, *Shekels, Dollars, and Sense: A Biblical Theology of Financial Stewardship* (UK: Trafford Publishing, 2006), 5.

Tithing with Zero New Testament Scriptural Backing

The question a prudent believer should ask themselves is this, "Where are all those New Testament passages that endorse tithing?" Did the Lord, our God Almighty, the giver of the Scriptures, forget to mention them? Apostle Paul and the other writers of the New Testament wrote on almost every aspect touching human's socio-economic and spiritual life, but tithes are never commanded or commended for followers of Christ.

This might probably be shocking to you. Do you know that from the time of Christ up till about the third century or so there was no historical record of tithe payment within the assembly of the believers of Christ? Tithing was smuggled into the Church sometime later. As Christianity moved further away from the true message of the gospel, this false doctrine (false with regards to the Christian faith, not Judaism) spread to the Protestant churches. Everyone became saturated with Malachi 3:8-10 as preachers tried to enrich themselves through the collection of tithes by instilling enormous fear into the hearts of the believers. For your information, the passage in Malachi 3 was never directed to or meant for the Church (we will see more on this later). Standing on scriptures that are not intended for the New Testament Church is standing on sinking sand.

Please note that we are not by any means suggesting here that all pastors who collect tithes are false teachers. No! Honestly speaking, some actually are. However, some have been led into that path by error, others by the spirit of covetousness.

Tithing: A Doctrine Driven by Emotion

In their defense of tithing, you'll hear preachers, and their members alike, say things like, "I know tithing works because it is the Word of God." And then you'll hear their companions, who practice tithing, but with nothing to show for it, shout, "Amen!" To this they add, "Praise God!" But, if we may recall, "Adulterers shall be put to death (Leviticus 20:10)" and "Thou shall not marry a Gentile/foreigner (Deuteronomy 7:3)," among others, are also the Word of God.

If we go by the reasoning of those who practice tithing in the Church, then we have to ensure that anyone who is caught in flagrant adultery today should be stoned to death with immediate effect for "it is the Word of God." We have only mentioned the two biblical examples above just to let you see the flaws in the reasoning of tithing advocates. Pro-tithe preachers throw out certain words to the people sitting in their pews with the intention of getting them trapped into their net. There are many things that are written in the Bible that are not addressed to everyone. That is why as followers of Christ, we are commanded to "show ourselves approved unto God" by "rightly dividing the Word of truth (2 Timothy 2:15)." Every passage of Scripture must be analyzed contextually through the biblical method of exegesis.

Another question asked by Bruce Wells we need to consider is this: if these other old covenant 'laws' no longer apply to us today, how come we have saved and are practicing today only the one that has to do with money? [6] Do you know that Malachi 3, the anchor passage often quoted by preachers to back up their teaching of tithing, was never addressed to the New Testament Church? Malachi 3 is just as out of place today as Galatians 3 would have been for the Levites in the Old Testament. These two books are from two different covenants, but order and doctrine don't matter anymore to the Church, Wells writes. We just use whatever passage we find in the Bible so far as it proves our point, Wells laments. [7]

Seeking God: The Testimony of a Pastor

A. Bruce Wells, a pastor, missionary and founder of Beautiful Feet Ministries, Inc., used to be a tithe payer and an acute defendant of it. However, wearied of seeing no fruits in his faithful payment of tithes, one evening Wells decided to seek the face of the Lord in a hotel room in Hannibal, MO, USA, where he had what he describes as *a Damascus Road Tithing Experience*. After hours of seeking the guidance of the Lord on the truth concerning tithing, Wells was visited by the Holy Spirit who directed him to connect the ordinances in Malachi 3:7-8 with the text in Colossians 2:14. Well's mouth dropped open as the Holy Spirit injected into his understanding that the ordinance of tithes in Malachi 3:7-8 was also nailed to the cross. [8] By this revelation, the scales fell off the pastor's eyes, and he was delivered from this religious burden.

For a comparative view, we will state the above two passages (supplementing each with an additional verse for the purpose of contextual understanding) here below:

---

[6] Wells, *The Great Tithing Debate*, xvii.
[7] Ibid., xviii.
[8] Ibid.

Malachi 3:7-8

⁷ Ever since the time of your ancestors you have turned away from my decrees and have not kept them. Return to me, and I will return to you," says the LORD Almighty. "But you ask, 'How are we to return?'

⁸ "Will a mere mortal rob God? Yet you rob me. "But you ask, 'How are we robbing you?' "In tithes and offerings.

Colossians 2:13-14

¹³ When you were dead in your sins and in the uncircumcision of your flesh, God made you alive with Christ. He forgave us all our sins,

¹⁴ having canceled the charge of our legal indebtedness, which stood against us and condemned us; he has taken it away, nailing it to the cross.

Misleading Ideas on Tithing

The invention of the tithing doctrine in the Church is predicated on two misleading ideas that have become a part of our normal Christian thinking enforced by the power of repetition, [9] Wells writes. The first is that we have been persuaded that tithing is not part of the Law, even though the Scriptures categorically affirm tithing to be a part of the Mosaic Law. Second, through sermons, we have been erroneously made to believe that 'tithing' and 'giving' are pretty much the same. They are not! They are COMPLETELY different!

Get Knowledge, Live Free!

In case the guilt of not paying tithes has become an issue of concern to you, or in case you have been struggling to be a better Christian through the payment of tithes to no avail, we suggest that you test everything that's being said in this book against the Scriptures (both Old and New Testaments). The Scriptures say that God's people perish because of the lack of knowledge. It is only when you are in possession of the right knowledge that you would be free from the curse of the law, that is, the guilt of tithing.

The Power of Money

Two friends who were engaged in an illegal business were shot by a policeman for attempting to escape. One of them received a bullet on the head but didn't die. The other died on the spot. Upon medical examination, it was revealed that the dead friend wasn't shot in the body but in the wallet.[10]

---

[9] Wells, *The Great Tithing Debate*, xviii.

[10] Adapted from Denis O. Wretlind, *Shekels, Dollars and Sense: A Biblical Theology of Financial Stewardship* (Oxford: Trafford Publishing, 2006), 1.

Being "shot in the wallet" is painful for every one of us. It is the singular reason why most pro-tithe pastors continue to advocate tithing. Besides tithing, this same phenomenon of being "shot in the wallet" accounts for many breakaways in homes, relationships, and corporate institutions.

Money is Power. The reason why ministers of the gospel will keep preaching about the smuggled tithing doctrine is because they are simply afraid that if the right to collect 10% of church members' income (while threatening them with punishment in case the members fail to comply) is taken away, they will lose all the money that would have enabled them have the best of life in ministry: buy the facilities they cherish, improve their personal lives and elevate their fame among peers in ministry. This is worldly thinking. Every minister of the gospel of the kingdom of God is called not to be of the world but to be the light of the world by reflecting Christ to the world through the continuation of the message that Christ had begun to teach and to do.

That said, even though it is quite evident from Scriptures that the New Testament does not support tithing in the Church in any way, tithe-collecting ministers would not acknowledge that. Pride and the love of money have kept them from admitting their error. So, in their desperation to get the tithes, they sugarcoat the tithing message with grace.

As a minister, you are not free to preach the true gospel of Christ until you are free from the seductive pull of money. Granted, we all need money to meet our needs, but we don't need money that comes to us through clandestine means. Money, described by the editors of Moody Monthly as civilization's indispensable middleman in the affairs of life, has the power to draw us to itself like a beacon. We must fight the good fight of faith to resist any clandestine gravitation toward money-making. Only by so doing can we preach a gospel that is free, true, and fair to all.

Thousands of Christians today are searching for real answers and for a Jesus that resembles the one described in the Bible, but unfortunately the Church is the worst place to look, Wells laments. [11]

---

[11] Wells, *The Great Tithing Debate*, xix.

Preliminary Hermeneutical Considerations

The primary goal of biblical exegesis is the discovery of *authorial intent*.[12] That is, whenever a person reads the Scriptures, their main focus should be to identify the intention of the author. What message, beyond the written letters, does the author really want to pass across? An important feature in exegesis that is vital in determining authorial intent is the issue of *primary* and *secondary meanings*. A common problem that usually arises in the course of studying a biblical passage is the failure to distinguish between the primary and secondary meanings of the passage in question. Primary meanings are "explicit propositions or imperatives" found in the text whilst secondary meanings are "derived only incidentally, by implications or by precedent."[13]

Let us take for our example Matthew 23:23:

> "Woe to you, teachers of the law and Pharisees, you hypocrites! You give a tenth of your spices—mint, dill and cumin. But you have neglected the more important matters of the law—justice, mercy and faithfulness. You should have practiced the latter, without neglecting the former."

Jesus was neither arguing for nor against the continuation of tithing by the Church.[14] Many advocates of tithing have used this passage as an inference that Jesus affirms tithing as a church doctrine. But that is not the primary meaning of the text. In determining authorial intent, the interpreter of Scripture must identify the primary meaning first. And only after then can they identify details that are incidental to the primary meaning. Therefore, elevating the secondary meaning of a text to a primary status, or having a textual interpretation that does not conform to the primary meaning, is compromising the original intent of the author. Here is the primary meaning of the text in question: Jesus was simply rebuking the Jews for not abiding to *priority*. The more important matters of the law must be attended first.

Another aspect that is associated with authorial intent is *context*. Context is an important restrainer, Croteau writes. It restrains the exegete from elevating the secondary meaning of a text Into Its primary meaning.

Another fatal error biblical interpreters make is equating <u>description</u> to <u>prescription</u>.[15] That the Bible describes an event in history does not

---

[12] Croteau, *You Mean I Don't Have to Tithe?* 4.
[13] Ibid., 5.
[14] Ibid.
[15] Ibid., 6.

mean that the Bible is prescribing that event to be practiced by men and women everywhere every time. The mere fact that the Bible describes Abram's giving of tithes to Melchizedek, for example, does not imply the Bible is prescribing or recommending that act to generations after Abraham. As an example, the Bible's description of Lot's daughters' sexual act with their father (Genesis 19:30-38) is not a prescription for practice by later generations.

Progressive Revelation

Another very important aspect to consider, especially relating to our topic on tithing, is the issue of *progressive revelation in the history of salvation.* [16] In accordance to the concept of progressive revelation, it seems worthwhile, Croteau writes, to conclude that "the New Testament is ultimately determinative for Christian morality and ethics, as well as all other matters." [17] While God himself did not evolve, His plan for Man's salvation did. The purpose of each writer of a biblical book was to capture the redemptive plan of God for God's people for that moment or dispensation. That is the reason why you would find a consistent development with respect to salvation in the writings of biblical authors, from the old to the new covenant. Putting everything together, Christ's work on the cross is FINAL for the salvation of humanity.

Let's give an example of progressive revelation. In Genesis 9:2-4, God told Noah that apart from meat that still has lifeblood in it, Noah could eat any animal for food.

Genesis 9:2-4

[2] The fear and dread of you will fall on all the beasts of the earth, and on all the birds in the sky, on every creature that moves along the ground, and on all the fish in the sea; they are given into your hands.

[3] Everything that lives and moves about will be food for you. Just as I gave you the green plants, I now give you everything.

[4] "But you must not eat meat that has its lifeblood still in it.

Later, in Leviticus 11:1-47 and Deuteronomy 14:7-19, certain animals were declared to be unclean, and, therefore, forbidden from being consumed.

Leviticus 11:4

[4] "'There are some that only chew the cud or only have a divided hoof, but

---

[16] Croteau, *You Mean I Don't Have to Tithe?* 6.
[17] Ibid.

you must not eat them. The camel, though it chews the cud, does not have a divided hoof; it is ceremonially unclean for you.

Deuteronomy 14:8

[8] The pig is also unclean; although it has a divided hoof, it does not chew the cud. You are not to eat their meat or touch their carcasses.

However, when we come down to Mark 7:18-20 and Acts 10:10-15 we see the restriction on unclean animals being lifted.

Acts 10:10-15

[10] He became hungry and wanted something to eat, and while the meal was being prepared, he fell into a trance.

[11] He saw heaven opened and something like a large sheet being let down to earth by its four corners.

[12] It contained all kinds of four-footed animals, as well as reptiles and birds.

[13] Then a voice told him, "Get up, Peter. Kill and eat."

[14] "Surely not, Lord!" Peter replied. "I have never eaten anything impure or unclean."

[15] The voice spoke to him a second time, "Do not call anything impure that God has made clean."

Mark 7:18-20

[18] "Are you so dull?" he asked. "Don't you see that nothing that enters a person from the outside can defile them?

[19] For it doesn't go into their heart but into their stomach, and then out of the body." (In saying this, Jesus declared all foods clean.)

[20] He went on: "What comes out of a person is what defiles them.

So, the revelation of God to His people has progressed over time. Now, the issue is not that God has changed over time, Croteau writes, but that the laws of the old covenant have found their fulfillment in Christ. [18]

In this book, we will be giving you biblical facts, not suggestions as advocates of tithing do, that tithing in the Church is a gross error, having been established therein either by the ignorance of the church leader or through manipulation of the congregation for the quest of amassing wealth or having control over the congregation.

The Purpose of this Book

It should be noted that the purpose of this book is not to attack ministers of the gospel. The author of this piece you're reading had

---

[18] Croteau, *You Mean I Don't Have to Tithe?* 7.

also been a victim of the tithe practice prior to his biblical revelation on the issue. We believe that not all ministers who collect tithes are fraudulent or manipulative. Some of them actually mean well for their congregation. They, like I, were taught by their mentors that tithing brings blessings, and they had believed this erroneous teaching throughout their lives unquestionably without any sound biblical scrutiny. It is commonly said, "Garbage in, garbage out!" These ministers who are really honest in their faith with God are now simply giving out what they had received. The intention of this book is to expose falsehood and, by so doing, re-orient believers of Christ to the truth.

God never admonishes us to have blind faith but He calls us all to seek understanding (Proverbs 4:5) based on His written Word, and not based on the doctrines of men. Contrary to popular belief, the faith that pleases God is possessed by those who have a firm understanding of the truth as expressed in God's Word. No wonder the Bible (in Romans 10:17) tell us that faith comes from hearing God's Word. But unless you understand what you hear, your hearing may be unfruitful. So, understanding what God, not men, says is supreme.

In this conviction, I presume to submit the following pages to the good sense of my fellow brethren of the Christian faith worldwide. In this book, I have endeavored to set before them the Biblical evidence why Tithing is not for the Church on account of the death and resurrection of our Lord and Savior, Jesus Christ.

2

THE HISTORY OF BIBLICAL TITHING

The Genesis of Tithing

In this chapter, we are going to examine for ourselves what the Bible really says about tithing. The Word of God is the only true yardstick for measuring and validating our theological and doctrinal views. We will start with the first book of the Old Testament where tithing was officially given to the children of Israel as an ordinance to be observed by them and their descendants. In the course of this chapter, we will also find out the following: why was the law of tithing given, to whom was it given specifically, who were the beneficiaries of the law, and, lastly, in what jurisdiction was the law to be applied?

From the Wilderness to the Promised Land

When the children of Israel were on their journey to the Promised Land (Canaan), the Lord God appeared unto Moses at Mount Sinai and, through Moses, gave a series of instructions relating to worship, which the Israelites were to follow as soon as they enter the Promised Land. A temple was to be built in the place where God would choose. In this temple, the Jewish people would gather every Sabbath to worship and praise their God who had revealed Himself to them as Yahweh.

The creation of a temple meant the creation of temple servants who would minister before Yahweh on behalf of the entire nation. The people that the LORD would choose to minister before Him were to dedicate themselves to the work of the temple. However, they were to be given some assistance by their fellow countrymen who were free from the work of the temple. This is where the creation of tithing came in, as will be explained in detail in the following pages.

When the people of Israel were being led away from Egypt to the Promised Land, at Sinai the Lord God told Moses to partition the land among eleven of the twelve tribes of Israel. Why eleven and not twelve? One out of the twelve tribes of Israel, the tribe of Levi, was chosen by God to constitute the servants of His temple. So, the Levites were given no land inheritance. The Lord God was to be their inheritance. What this means is that whatever was brought to God by the non-Levitical tribes belonged to the Levites.

Furthermore, from the tribe of Levi, the house of Aaron was chosen to constitute the priesthood. The Levites in general (made up of both the priestly and non-priestly classes) were forbidden from owning lands. Since the Levites did not get, and could not own, any land inheritance to cultivate crops or graze cattle for their daily living, the Lord God, therefore, commanded the non-Levitical tribes (that got land inheritance) to give to the Levites a tithe (10%) of their cultivated crops (and livestock). This was equated to 'bringing a tithe to the Lord.' This was the foundation of tithing.

Now, we will look at those biblical passages where the things we have just said above are written. We will label them in points form.

BIBLICAL TITHING IN CONTEXT

A. THE REGULATIONS THAT LED TO THE CREATION OF THE TITHING LAW

Point #1:

✓ **The Levites Chosen as Ministers of the Temple.**

Deuteronomy 10:8-9

8 At that time the LORD set apart the tribe of Levi to carry the ark of the covenant of the LORD, to stand before the LORD to minister and to pronounce blessings in his name, as they still do today.

9 That is why the Levites have no share or inheritance among their fellow Israelites; the LORD is their inheritance, as the LORD your God told them.)

In connection to God's plan of building a temple of worship, the tribe of Levi was separated by God to minister before Him at the temple on behalf of the entire nation of Israel. As a result, the Levites were forbidden from having as inheritance any allotment from the distributed land of promise, Canaan land.

Point #2:

✓ Aaron and His Descendants Chosen as Priests.

Numbers 18:1

¹ The LORD said to Aaron, "You, your sons and your family are to bear the responsibility for offenses connected with the sanctuary, and you and your sons alone are to bear the responsibility for offenses connected with the priesthood.

Aaron and his descendants were then chosen to be the LORD's priests. You may be asking, "Why was Aaron, and not Moses, chosen as priest?" That's a good question! But the reason for Aaron's choice over Moses was simply because right from the time of Adam, the male head or first son of every Jewish family was the legitimate priest of that family. The male head built altars upon which sacrifices were made to God on behalf of his family. This system of priesthood was known as **the priesthood of the firstborn.** Aaron being the first son in the house of Amram (Miriam-Aaron-Moses) made him the natural priest of that house.

However, as shown in Numbers 18:1 above, the priesthood of the firstborn became obsolete with respect to the building of individual family altars. Each Jewish family was no longer permitted to raise a family altar. Aaron and his sons, who were all descendants of the tribe of Levi, were chosen by the Lord to constitute the priesthood not just for that tribe but for the entire nation of Israel. This national priesthood is commonly referred to as *the Aaronic Priesthood*. The chosen priests were to bear the iniquity of their priesthood, and of the sanctuary on behalf of the nation.

The priestly appointment of Aaron and his descendants could also be found in 1 Chronicles 23:13 shown below:

1 Chronicles 23:13

¹³ The sons of Amram: Aaron and Moses. Aaron was set apart, he and his descendants forever, to consecrate the most holy things, to offer sacrifices before the LORD, to minister before him and to pronounce blessings in his name forever.

Today, you may even find some Christians building personal/family

altars for worship. Most of them have been taught so by their 'pastor."
We would not throw much blame on those who propagate such
teachings on the building of personal/family altars because they
might have had good intentions but were simply misled due to their
ignorance of the biblical position regarding altar-building. However, if
you're reading this, what you need to take note as a child of God
under the new covenant of Christ is this: God does not require you to
build any external temple for worship. You are the temple of God (1
Corinthians 3:16; 6:19). That's the temple He abides in, not the one
that's made with human hands.

1 Corinthians 6:19-20

[19] Do you not know that your bodies are temples of the Holy Spirit, who is in
you, whom you have received from God? You are not your own;

[20] you were bought at a price. Therefore honor God with your bodies.

Point #3:

✓   Non-priestly Levites Chosen as Waiters/Assistants to the Priests.

1 Chronicles 23:27-28

[27] According to the last instructions of David, the Levites were counted from
those twenty years old or more.

[28] The duty of the Levites was to help Aaron's descendants in the service of
the temple of the LORD: to be in charge of the courtyards, the side rooms, the
purification of all sacred things and the performance of other duties at the
house of God.

The descendants of Levi (apart from the house of Aaron that
constituted the priesthood), were chosen by the Lord to assist the
priests in the Temple. They are not a part of the priesthood. Their work
is simply to provide assistance to the priests.

As we have seen in the above passages, the descendants of the tribe
of Levi in Israel, be they priests or assistants to the priests, were the
ones chosen by the Lord to work in His temple.

The offices of the priestly and non-priestly Levites in the old covenant,
and their respective relations with respect to the tithes offered by the
non-Levitical tribes disprove any claims of pastors being the Church
equivalent of "the Levites in Israel" for the purpose of tithe collection.
Even if we assume the claim to be true, this would not yet validate the
collection of 10% worth the monthly income of members of their
congregation, as we are going to see in subsequent pages.

Let us assume that pastors hold the office of the old covenant priests in Judaism. The fact that pastors who make such a claim are not traceable descendants of the Levitical tribe of Israel betrays their claim. All Jewish priests are descendants of the tribe of Levi, which is traceable in the land of Israel. One can only become a Levite by birth, not by any spiritual affiliations or connections.

Point #4:

✓ The Levites Restricted from Land Inheritance.

Numbers 18:20-21

[20] The LORD said to Aaron, "You will have no inheritance in their land, nor will you have any share among them; I am your share and your inheritance among the Israelites."

[21] "I give to the Levites all the tithes in Israel as their inheritance in return for the work they do while serving at the tent of meeting."

To enable them to be fully committed in the work of the Temple, the Levites were restricted from acquiring any property from the distributed land. In verse 20 above, the Lord reiterates to Aaron that the Levites shall have no allotment in the distributed land. The Lord assured Aaron that He shall be their inheritance. This inheritance is specified in verse 21 to be *tithe*: "I have given the children of Levi all the tenth in Israel for an inheritance." Therefore, the tithe that was given to the Levites was a form of compensation or replacement for the land inheritance they would have normally acquired as a legitimate tribe in Israel.

B. IMPORTANT POINTS TO NOTE ABOUT "TITHING"

Point #1:

✓ Tithing was a commandment/law.

Leviticus 27:30, 34

[30] "A tithe of everything from the land, whether grain from the soil or fruit from the trees, belongs to the LORD; it is holy to the LORD."

[34] These are the commands the LORD gave Moses at Mount Sinai for the Israelites.

Given that the Levites were forbidden from having any land inheritance, the Lord God promised that He was going to be their inheritance instead. So, the Lord commanded the other eleven (non-Levitical) tribes to offer to Him tithes, which were given to the Levites, and first fruits, vows, sacrifices, sin offerings, etc., which were given to the priests (Aaron and his descendants). It was for this reason that tithing was officially promulgated as a divine law to be adhered to by the children of Israel.

After the Lord God had instructed the non-Levitical tribes of Israel to give tithes unto the Levites (Leviticus 27:30), the Bible specifies in the last verse (vv. 35) that "these are the commandments" implying that everything that had been spoken before this verse were commandments. The instruction to tithe occurs in verse 30. Therefore, tithing is a commandment or law.

Unlike followers of the Law of Moses, followers of Christ operate under the new covenant. Under this covenant, they are under GRACE, and not under the Law anymore. The laws, including tithing, have ALL been nailed to the cross by the messiah, Jesus Christ. And that's the reason why Tithing is not for the Church.

With regards to tithing being a law, and the hypocrisy of ministers of the gospel to demand tithes from believers, William Hincks writes:

> "The tithes are strictly a part of the Levitical law of the Jews, for they were required to be offered as heave offerings before they could be applied to use, and the obligation to pay them was on **Israelites only**, to a particular class of men consecrated to God in a peculiar manner, so that they must stand or fall with the other parts of the Hebrew ritual. That law having been abolished by Christ, no claim can now properly be founded upon it, and if it could be requisite to obey it in any one point (I here oppose the ritual to the moral laws which are established and extended by Christianity) the obligation would extend to all: but the abolition of the ritual law in other points is acknowledged and maintained. How then are those to be well acquitted of hypocrisy, who uphold it in one particular, in which their own interest is concerned, whilst they reject it in all others?" [19]

Point #2:

Tithe Was An Inheritance to the Levites.

Numbers 18:24

[24] "Instead, I give to the Levites as their inheritance the tithes that the Israelites present as an offering to the LORD. That is why I said concerning them: 'They will have no inheritance among the Israelites.'"

Since the Levites were forbidden from acquiring lands, the tithes of the

[19] William Hincks, *The Claims of the Clergy to Tithes and Other Church Revenues, 2nd Ed.* (London: Effingham Wilson, 1830), 13-14.

non-Levitical tribes of Israel were given to them as their inheritance as shown in Numbers 18:24 above.

The setting is totally different with the New Testament Church. In the Church, the priesthood is not attached to any particular tribe. The believers are all priests; their priesthood is referred to as **The Priesthood of All Believers**. Jesus Christ is their High Priest. No one is forbidden from working outside of the church institution; no one is forbidden from owning private properties. Therefore, the believers of Christ have no divine mandate to give tithes as a compensation or inheritance to their fellow brethren who minister God's Word unto them. However, they can support the minister or any other brethren who are in need. On the priesthood of followers of Christ, Kelly writes:

"In the Church Age, all Christians are unconditionally constituted a 'kingdom of priests' (1 Pet. 2:9; Rev. 1:6), the distinction which Israel failed to achieve by works. The priesthood of the Christian is, therefore, a birthright, just as every descendant of Aaron was born to the priesthood (Heb. 5:1)."[20]

Point #3:

✓ Tithe Is Given from Crops or Livestock.

A. Tithe from Crops

Leviticus 27:30

[30] "A tithe of everything from the land, whether grain from the soil or fruit from the trees, belongs to the LORD; it is holy to the LORD."

Deuteronomy 14:22

[22] Be sure to set aside a tenth of all that your fields produce each year.

As shown in the two passages above, the tithe was given from harvested crops and not from the monthly income or salary one acquired from their business, which had nothing to do with the ground or field.

B. Tithe from Livestock

Leviticus 27:32

[32] Every tithe of the herd and flock—every tenth animal that passes under the shepherd's rod—will be holy to the LORD.

---

[20] Kelly, *Should the Church Teach Tithing?* 138.

In addition to crops grown in the land of Israel, the children of Israel were also told to offer a tenth of their livestock to the Lord as tithe. Again, they weren't told to offer 10% of the money they realized from the sale of their flocks. No. The Lord God demanded a tenth of the flock, not a tenth of the sale money of the flock.

Point #4:

✓   **Tithe Is <u>Not Money</u>!**

Leviticus 27:30

[30] "A tithe of everything from the land, whether grain from the soil or fruit from the trees, belongs to the LORD; it is holy to the LORD."

As shown above, the children of Israel were strictly commanded to bring tithes from the harvested crops that were planted on the land, which they had acquired as a gift from the LORD God. The content of the tithe was limited to "the produce of the land," which involved livestock (as the land was used for pasture). They were never told to bring to the Lord a tithe from their income. Therefore, tithe <u>is not</u> 10% of the believer's monthly salary as many have been taught to believe. *Tithe was never about money.* It was agricultural food (or livestock), which was meant for the Levites and the poor within the believing community.

Nehemiah 10:37 re-emphasizes the fact that tithing had nothing to do with money. The expression "the tithes of our ground" indicates that tithe was given not from one's income but from the agricultural crops that were planted on the land of Israel.

Nehemiah 10:37

[37] "Moreover, we will bring to the storerooms of the house of our God, to the priests, the first of our ground meal, of our grain offerings, of the fruit of all our trees and of our new wine and olive oil. And we will bring a tithe of our crops to the Levites, for it is the Levites who collect the tithes in all the towns where we work."

Where Tithing Involved Money

Deuteronomy 14:24-26

[24] But if that place is too distant and you have been blessed by the LORD your God and cannot carry your tithe (because the place where the LORD will choose to put his Name is so far away),

[25] then exchange your tithe for silver, and take the silver with you and go to the place the LORD your God will choose.

²⁶ Use the silver to buy whatever you like: cattle, sheep, wine or other fermented drink, or anything you wish. Then you and your household shall eat there in the presence of the LORD your God and rejoice.

The only place where money was involved in tithing was in a situation whereby the Jew lived quite a distance away from the Temple in Jerusalem. And this was only connected to the Festival Tithe. When a Jew lived far away from the Temple, the Jew was told to sell their tithe in their place of residence, and take the money with them to Jerusalem. At Jerusalem, they could then use the money to buy material items of their choice for their annual feast celebrations. This is illustrated in Deuteronomy 14:24-26 above.

Point #5:

✓   Tithing Was Limited to Judaism and the Land of Israel.

Leviticus 27:30, 34:

³⁰ "A tithe of everything from the land, whether grain from the soil or fruit from the trees, belongs to the LORD; it is holy to the LORD."

³⁴ These are the commands the LORD gave Moses at Mount Sinai for the Israelites.

The command to tithe was given exclusively to the nation of Israel. The reasons abound.
First, it was to compensate the Levites in general for their work in the temple.

Unlike pastors in the Church, the Levites were strictly forbidden from acquiring lands as personal properties or from doing any other work for their sustenance apart from the work of the Temple. Apostle Paul's statement in 2 Thessalonians 3:7-8 could be taken as an advice to pastors to have a job outside the local church so they do not become a burden to the believers of the church:

2 Thessalonians 3:7-8

⁷ For you yourselves know how you ought to follow our example. We were not idle when we were with you,

⁸ nor did we eat anyone's food without paying for it. On the contrary, we worked night and day, laboring and toiling so that we would not be a burden to any of you.

Second, the Levites were the only group of people who were appointed by God to collect tithes, and this tribe is limited to national Israel. The Church is made up of Gentiles. There is no tribe of Levi among the Gentiles. Clearly, the Levites are all descendants of Levi. In their greed to receive tithes, I have heard some church leaders say a bizarre thing like "Pastors are the spiritual Levites of the Church."

Third, the Levites did not receive any tithes that came from a land other than the land of Israel. In fact, after their return from exile, the requirement to tithe was narrowed down. The land was subdivided into three separate zones of holiness. The second and third tithes, which did not come from the land of Jordan, could not be allowed into the temple. [21]

The clause in Numbers 18:21, "I have given the children of Levi **all the tenth in Israel**" implies that tithing was limited to the land of Israel.

Point #6:

✓   The Jews Did Not Tithe Until They Had Entered Canaan.

Deuteronomy 12:1

[1] These are the decrees and laws you must be careful to follow in the land that the LORD, the God of your ancestors, has given you to possess—as long as you live in the land.

Before the laws were given, the Jews were told that those laws were to be put into practice only when they had entered the Promised Land. Among the given laws was the law of tithing (Deuteronomy 12:6). Do you know that the Jews did not pay tithes for the entire 40 years that they spent in the wilderness? Yes, that is a historical fact. And that was because God's people were abiding by God's Law. They were only to practice tithing in the Promised Land, and nowhere else. So, tithing was integrally connected to <u>the land of Israel</u>.

Point #7:

✓   Priests Received Only 1% of the Levitical Tithe.

Numbers 18:25-28

[25] The LORD said to Moses,

[26] "Speak to the Levites and say to them: 'When you receive from the Israelites the tithe I give you as your inheritance, you must present a tenth of that tithe as the LORD's offering.

---

[21] Kelly, *Should the Church Teach Tithing?* 42.

²⁷ Your offering will be reckoned to you as grain from the threshing floor or juice from the winepress.

²⁸ In this way you also will present an offering to the LORD from all the tithes you receive from the Israelites. From these tithes you must give the LORD's portion to Aaron the priest.

When the Levites received tithes from the non-Levites, the tithes of the Levites were considered as the Levites' grain field (Numbers 18:27). As a result, the Levites (who were made up of singers, porters, etc. serving the priests at the Temple) were also commanded to give to the priests a tithe of the tithes they had received from the non-Levites (Numbers 18:26, 28). This is called **the tithe of tithes**.

In principle, the priests received only one percent of the tithes that the children of Israel (non-Levites) were commanded to give to the LORD God. This regulation is also mentioned in Nehemiah 12:47 shown here-below:

Nehemiah 12:47

⁴⁷ So in the days of Zerubbabel and of Nehemiah, all Israel contributed the daily portions for the musicians and the gatekeepers. They also set aside the portion for the other Levites, and the Levites set aside the portion for the descendants of Aaron.

Since the Levitical tithe was earmarked as the Levites' grain field, and given that a tithe is normally demanded from every owner of grain field in the land of Israel, the Levites gave a tenth of their tithes, known as *heave offering,* otherwise called *tithe of tithes,* to the priests. Since the priests did not receive any tithes from the non-Levites to be considered as a grain field, they were not required by law to give any tithes.

Point #8:

✓   Tithes were stored in a Storehouse.

2 Chronicles 31:11-12

¹¹ Hezekiah gave orders to prepare storerooms in the temple of the LORD, and this was done.

¹² Then they faithfully brought in the contributions, tithes and dedicated gifts. Konaniah, a Levite, was the overseer in charge of these things, and his brother Shimei was next in rank.

When King Hezekiah saw the great heap of tithes, he gave an order for a separate chamber to be built where tithes could be stored. The tithes were to be used to assist the poor, the widows, the orphans and the strangers.

When you're in need, walk to your local church, we guarantee you that you'll barely find a storehouse in the church auditorium from which the poor, orphans, widows, and strangers of that church could be served with material resources. Most church leaders are simply interested in receiving and not in giving to the poor. There are even reports of church members, some of who consist of tithe payers, who go to meet their local pastor in a time of need only to be given a re-appointment or turned down categorically.

Point #9:

✓ **The people gave tithes to the Levites, not to the Temple**

Nehemiah 10:37

[37] "Moreover, we will bring to the storerooms of the house of our God, to the priests, the first of our ground meal, of our grain offerings, of the fruit of all our trees and of our new wine and olive oil. And we will bring a tithe of our crops to the Levites, for it is the Levites who collect the tithes in all the towns where we work."

Point #10:

✓ **Only the Priests/Levites were to bring tithes into the Temple**

Nehemiah 10:38

[38] A priest descended from Aaron is to accompany the Levites when they receive the tithes, and the Levites are to bring a tenth of the tithes up to the house of our God, to the storerooms of the treasury.

The children of Israel were not commanded to bring their tithes into the storehouse of the Temple. They were rather told to take their tithes to the Levitical cities (rural towns, NIV) as shown in Nehemiah 10:37 here above. It was the workers of the Temple (the priests and Levites) who were commanded to bring into the Temple a tithe of the tithes they had received from the people, as shown in Nehemiah 10:38 above. So, Malachi 3:10 was surely referring to the priests and Levites when he said, "Bring all the tithes into the storehouse so there will be enough food in my Temple."

Point #11:

✓ **Levites could eat their tithes in their place of choice.**

Numbers 18:31

[31] You Levites and your families may eat this food anywhere you wish, for it is your compensation for serving in the Tabernacle.

After heaving a tenth from the tithes, which they gave to the priests, the Levites could eat the remainder with their household in the place of their choice for it is their reward for their service in the tabernacle of the congregation. This is a clear proof that the biblical tithe was never meant to be used as project money in the house of God. It was given to the Levites as their inheritance for their service in the temple of God. And, to be more precise, the tithe was given to the Levites to meet their daily needs since they were given no lands upon which they could cultivate crops. The picture is completely different with pastors in the Church.

Point #12:

✓ **Tithe was never used for the maintenance of the Temple.**

Nehemiah 10:32-33

[32] "We assume the responsibility for carrying out the commands to give a third of a shekel each year for the service of the house of our God:

[33] for the bread set out on the table; for the regular grain offerings and burnt offerings; for the offerings on the Sabbaths, at the New Moon feasts and at the appointed festivals; for the holy offerings; for sin offerings to make atonement for Israel; and for all the duties of the house of our God."

In Judaism, the tithe or the sale of a tithe was never used to build, maintain the Temple of God or carry out any Temple-related projects. For the maintenance of the Temple, the Jews were strictly commanded to pay the Temple Tax, which was set at one-eighth of an ounce (i.e. 3.54 grams) of silver as shown above.

It is very uncommon for church leaders to put forward the maintenance of the church building as a legitimate reason why they should collect tithes. As an accountant in a Douala-based (Cameroon) charismatic church, I have been a witness to this phenomenon. Pastors will tell you that the tithes they collect are to enable them build, furnish the church facility, or carry out a new project therein.

The attitude of pastors to justify the collection of tithes from Christ's followers can only lead us into asking this question: "Do pastors, who should be the shepherds of Christ's followers, really understand what tithe was meant for?" The biblical tithe was never meant for church projects. Fact! Tithe was the property right of descendants from the Jewish tribe of Levi given to them by law as a replacement for the land inheritance they were forbidden from acquiring. Tithe is not the property right of any pastors or church members. Neither is tithe meant for building or maintaining a church facility. Tithe or tithing has nothing to do with the Church of Christ. Christ himself had fulfilled the requirement to tithe commanded in the Law of Moses.

Point #13:

✓ Tithes were brought to a single place (Jerusalem) by all Israel.

Deuteronomy 12:5-6

5 But you are to seek the place the LORD your God will choose from among all your tribes to put his Name there for his dwelling. To that place you must go;

6 there bring your burnt offerings and sacrifices, your tithes and special gifts, what you have vowed to give and your freewill offerings, and the firstborn of your herds and flocks.

The Jews, irrespective of their place of residence, were commanded to offer their tithes unto the place the Lord God would choose. When they got into the Promised Land, that place came to be the Temple at Jerusalem. So, Jews living far off from Jerusalem had to carry their tithes into Jerusalem. However, a modification of this aspect of the law was made (see "Where Tithing Involved Money," page 29).

With respect to the Church of Christ, the situation is completely different for the following reasons:

- The Church does not have any common Temple, which the LORD God has chosen out of all the nations of the earth to put His name there (see Deuteronomy 12:5). It is into this common physical Temple that tithes are commanded to be brought. The Church does not have such a Temple into which believers worldwide should deposit their tithes.

- The Jews, irrespective of their location, were commanded to drop their tithes at the Temple in Jerusalem because the LORD God resided in that Temple. In the Church, the LORD's Temple is not a physical external structure. The Temple of the LORD is located in the body of the believer of Christ. Therefore, if the believer of Christ were to practice the law of tithing in a conforming manner to the Law of Moses, then the tithe of the believer of Christ ought to remain within his body (God's Temple)

and not taken out of it.

- Tithes were connected to Jewish ceremonial worship. The Church is free of such worship. As a consequence, the Church has not been commanded to practice tithing.

Point #14

✓ **There was transparency in the collection of tithes.**

2 Chronicles 31:8-10

[8] When Hezekiah and his officials came and saw the heaps, they praised the LORD and blessed his people Israel.

[9] Hezekiah asked the priests and Levites about the heaps;

[10] and Azariah the chief priest, from the family of Zadok, answered, "Since the people began to bring their contributions to the temple of the LORD, we have had enough to eat and plenty to spare, because the LORD has blessed his people, and this great amount is left over."

When the children of Israel brought their tithes to the temple, there was a system of transparency in place. Everyone could see what had been brought as tithes, including the king, Hezekiah, and the princes. When King Hezekiah saw the huge heap of tithes, he was filled with awe, and blessed the name of the Lord. Today, churches barely give true accountability of what they had collected from the congregation. That is not the spirit of truth. With respect to accountability, I did use the adjective "true" here for emphasis purposes. As a trained accountant, I can say this about accountability. Whenever you find someone hesitating or delaying in giving accountability of a project, know that there is something they have hidden, or are hiding, under the carpet. They are not transparent.

Point #15 (Deuteronomy 24:19-21):

✓ **The tithe of the land did not include ALL of the land.**

Deuteronomy 24:19-22

[19] When you are harvesting in your field and you overlook a sheaf, do not go back to get it. Leave it for the foreigner, the fatherless and the widow, so that the LORD your God may bless you in all the work of your hands.

[20] When you beat the olives from your trees, do not go over the branches a second time. Leave what remains for the foreigner, the fatherless and the widow.

[21] When you harvest the grapes in your vineyard, do not go over the vines again. Leave what remains for the foreigner, the fatherless and the widow.

[22] Remember that you were slaves in Egypt. That is why I command you to do this.

The ordinance of gleanings required landowners not to harvest the corners of their fields, and not to pick up what has fallen after the harvest. These were reserved for the orphans, widows, and strangers of the land, and were not to be counted in the quota that was to be given as tithe.

Point #16:

✓   **A tithe can neither be manually selected nor changed.**

Leviticus 27:33

[33] "You may not pick and choose between good and bad animals, and you may not substitute one for another. But if you do exchange one animal for another, then both the original animal and its substitute will be considered holy and cannot be bought back."

In presenting the tithe of his flock, the owner is not to select the good ones from the bad ones or vice-versa. He must only present as tithe the tenth animal that passes under the rod, as we have just seen here above.

The tenth animal that passes under the rod is devoted unto the Lord. And what has been devoted unto the Lord is *holy*, and, therefore, cannot be recalled or used for any other purposes.

The Jews were strictly forbidden from making any changes on the animal tithe. If the tithe turned out to be a female, it could not be switched for a male, and vice versa. If it were an unblemished animal, it could not be replaced with a blemished one, and vice-versa. If that happened to have been done, then both the replacement and the original tithe (that is, the tenth animal that had passed under the rod) must remain the property of the Lord for they are holy. This ordinance was put in place to prevent the Jews from changing the tithes of their flock at all cost.

How the Tithe Was Chosen:

"Whatsoever passeth under the rod"

Leviticus 27:32:

[32] Count off every tenth animal from your herds and flocks and set them apart for the lord as holy.

According to rabbinical tradition, when the Jew had to give a tithe of his lambs or calves, he would gather them together and make a narrow gate so that two cannot pass through the gate at the same time. As the shepherd bleats, the lambs hear his voice and make their way out of the gate one after the other to meet their master. The shepherd cannot choose which lamb passes through the gate; the lambs must be allowed to pass by themselves, hence, the expression, "whatsoever passeth under the rod."

As the lambs pass through the narrow gate one after the other, the shepherd counts them with a rod, one, two, three, etc., and the tenth lamb is marked for the tithe by touching it with the same rod that had been dipped in vermillion. [22] The tenth animal must be marked as the tithe irrespective of whether it is a male or female, blemished or unblemished. It is then offered to the priest. [23]

Ezekiel 20:37 (KJV) uses the same expression when the Lord, through the prophet, Ezekiel, said to the children of Israel that, in order to bring them into His covenant, He will cause them to "pass under the rod." Therefore, "Passing under the rod" is a terminology that is used to depict the separation of a thing for the purpose of dedication to the Most High God. And whatever passes under the rod is considered holy unto the Lord.

Point #17 (Leviticus 27:32)

✓   The Tithe was not necessarily the best portion.

Some have taught that tithes were always the best, but as we have seen in the selection process of the tithe (see Leviticus 27:32-34) with regards to animals, the tithe is simply the tenth animal that "passes under the rod" and not necessarily the best as the animals are allowed to pass through the narrow gate by themselves; they're not chosen by hand. The outcome of the tithe (good or bad) was a matter of probability, not human choice. Whether the tithe was good or bad, it was sanctified to be "holy unto the LORD." The Jew cannot determine beforehand which of the animals would be given as tithe. The expression, "whatsoever passeth under the rod, the tenth shall be holy unto the LORD" clearly explains the fact that tithing has to do with the tenth portion, not necessarily the best portion. This is contrary

---

22 Barnes' Notes on the Bible, *Leviticus 27:32;* Internet; accessed 21 August 2020; available from biblehub.com.

23 Ellicott's Commentary for English Readers, *Leviticus 27:32,* Internet; accessed 21 August 2020; available from biblehub.com.

to popular thinking.

Regarding the claim that the tithe was always the best, Kelly comments:

> The myth exists that tithes were always the BEST. This is not a biblical truth! Actually, the food tithe given to the Levites was the TENTH, and not necessarily the best; also, the animal tithes given to the Levites was EVERY TENTH, not the best (Lev. 27:32-33). However, when the Levites gave their tenth of the tithe to the priests, only that portion was to be the BEST. [24]

Point #18 (Leviticus 27:32)

✓ There were three types of Tithe.

There were three types of tithe: the Levitical Tithe, the Festival Tithe, and the Charity Tithe. Hardly will you hear this being preached from the pulpit for manipulative reasons.

THE THREE TYPES OF TITHE

1) The Levitical Tithe (*Ma'aser Rishon*)

This is the first tithe. In Numbers 18:21, 24, the children of Israel were specifically told to give a tithe of the increase of their crops and cattle to the Levites for the work the Levites do in the temple of the LORD (see Point #2, page 26).

Please note that in this book when we refer to *tithe* or *tithing*, we are refering to the Levitical Tithe since the payment of this tithe is the doctrine that is currently being practiced in most churches.

2) The Festival Tithe *(Ma'aser Sheni)*

This is the second tithe. In Deuteronomy 14:22-23, the LORD God commanded the people of Israel to set aside a tithe from the produce of their land, which was to be taken to the Temple in Jerusalem to be eaten together with their fellow brethren during their appointed annual feasts.

Deuteronomy 14:22-23

[22] Be sure to set aside a tenth of all that your fields produce each year.

---

[24] Kelly, *Should the Church Teach Tithing?* 37.

²³ Eat the tithe of your grain, new wine and olive oil, and the firstborn of your herds and flocks in the presence of the LORD your God at the place he will choose as a dwelling for his Name, so that you may learn to revere the LORD your God always.

3)   The Charity Tithe (*Ma'aser Ani*)

This is the third tithe, also known as the Poor Man's Tithe. The Israelites were also commanded to set aside, at the end of every three years, a separate tithe for the poor, orphans, widows, strangers, including Levites who did not have enough resources.

Deuteronomy 14:28-29

²⁸ At the end of every three years, bring all the tithes of that year's produce and store it in your towns,

²⁹ so that the Levites (who have no allotment or inheritance of their own) and the foreigners, the fatherless and the widows who live in your towns may come and eat and be satisfied, and so that the LORD your God may bless you in all the work of your hands.

Important to Note:

✓   **The priests/Levites were not full-time ministers.**

(1 Chronicles 24:1-19)

During the reform of King David, the priests (sixteen sons of Eleazar and eight sons of Ithamar) were divided by lot into twenty-four divisions. They took turns to minister in the Temple of the Lord. If you do the math, you'll realize that each lot serves in the Temple for approximately two weeks only in a whole calendar year (see 1 Chronicles 24:1-19).

The Levites (288 in number), likewise, were divided into twenty-four lots of twelve each. They took turns in their service in the Temple (see 1 Chronicles 25:1-31).

Overleaf is a statistics of the Levites (men, thirty years and above) who worked in different sectors of the country. This statistics was published following the census of King David.

STATISTICS OF THE MALE POPULATION OF LEVITES ⩾ 30 YEARS	
Temple Workers	24,000
Officers and Judges [civil & religious]	6,000
Porters	4,000
Musicians	4,000
Total	**38,000**

✓ Some Priests Served in the Army

(1 Chronicles 27:1, 5)

Also, note that, unlike pastors of the Church, in the Old Testament, some priests were also part of the army. Benaiah, for example, the son of Jehoiada the high priest was commander of a battalion of twenty-four thousand soldiers, as shown below:

1 Chronicles 27:1, 5

[1] This is the list of the Israelites—heads of families, commanders of thousands and commanders of hundreds, and their officers, who served the king in all that concerned the army divisions that were on duty month by month throughout the year. Each division consisted of 24,000 men.

[5] The third army commander, for the third month, was Benaiah son of Jehoiada the priest. He was chief and there were 24,000 men in his division.

It should be recalled that by default the duty post of the priests and Levites is the Temple of God. It will be surprising to note that not all priests lived at Jerusalem, the holy city, where the Temple was located. Some of the priests and Levites were also among the nine-tenth of the people who dwelt in their various homes in the cities of Judah, as shown below:

Nehemiah 11:3, 20

[3] These are the provincial leaders who settled in Jerusalem (now some Israelites, priests, Levites, temple servants and descendants of Solomon's servants lived in the towns of Judah, each on their own property in the various towns,

[20] The rest of the Israelites, with the priests and Levites, were in all the towns of Judah, each on their ancestral property.

You may want to ask, "What were the priests and Levites doing in their various cities in Judah?" Well, our analysis under 1 Chronicles showed that the 24 divisions of priests and Levites took turns to serve in the Temple. We can only speculate that the priests and Levites living in Judah travelled from time to time to minister at the Jerusalem Temple. In case our speculation is not the case, then they might have been engaged in some farming or cattle-rearing activity in Judah. That notwithstanding, what is evident is that not all priests worked permanently in the Temple.

In conclusion, what we can say based on the data we have is that the priests and Levites did not work full-time in the Temple at Jerusalem. They worked in a Lot-shift system with each individual working for as little as two weeks in a whole year.

The reason we are mentioning all these biblical facts is to counteract the popular argument advanced by some ministers of the gospel that the Levites/priests received tithes because they were full-time workers in the house of God. Therefore, they argue that they, too, being full-time ministers, are entitled to the tithes. We have just debunked this lie by showing that the priests/Levites were not full-time workers, and that not all priests/Levites did serve in the Temple of the Lord. Some held positions in the king's government; others were part of the military.

3

THE EARLY CHURCH & MONEY

Before we begin this chapter, it should be remarked that no mention or practice of tithing occurred in the Church for at least the first three hundred and fifty years of its existence. The early Church collected freewill offerings from which the poor were taken care of.

A case worth mentioning here can be found in Acts 4:32-35. Knowing they were not mandated to pay tithes, the believers brought their individual resources to be used by their fellow brethren. If the payment of tithes was a Christian doctrine, mindful of the faithfulness of the early Disciples of Christ, the application of the command to tithe as instructed by the Law of Moses would have been top on their agenda.

Unfortunately, consumed by greed, some pastors have called on the members of their congregation to surrender their properties such as land, houses, etc., to the local church invoking what happened in Acts 4:32ff as a biblical justification for their call. But the Scripture must not be taken out of its context. In Acts 4:32ff, what the disciples in Jerusalem did was that they sold their properties, brought the money to the local church, which was divided equally among the brethren, as shown below:

Acts 4:32-35

32 All the believers were united in heart and mind. And they felt that what they owned was not their own, so they shared everything they had.

33 The apostles testified powerfully to the resurrection of the Lord Jesus, and God's

great blessing was upon them all.

³⁴ There were no needy people among them, because those who owned land or houses would sell them

³⁵ and bring the money to the apostles to give to those in need.

POINTS TO NOTE!

Regarding the above passage, kindly note the following points:

1. The believers were of one heart and of one soul (vv. 32). That means they were fully satisfied with the composition of the church, its doctrines, leaders, and the way the church was administered.

2. They knew they did not really own what they had (vv. 32). It was given to them to share with those who didn't have. Thanks to this conviction, they shared what they had with the needy in their midst. Note that they were not told to do so by their leaders.

3. They sold lands or houses, brought the money and laid it at the apostles' feet (vv. 34-35). They did this not because it was commanded anywhere in the Bible, but because of Point 1 above. In addition, they trusted their leaders to be good stewards who would not mismanage what was given to them for the sake of the poor.

4. Here comes the key text in the above passage. The money was given to the apostles *to be distributed to the believers of the church in question according to their needs* (vv. 35). Thus, the purpose of the money that was laid at the apostles' feet was to cater for the needs of the believers in the church at Jerusalem. It was not given to the apostles as a 'prophet offering,' it was not given to the apostles to buy a church land or building, or to open up a small profit-making business for the church. The believers had fellowship in private homes, and they were contented with that arrangement.

Why Did the Disciples at Jerusalem Sell Their Properties?

But why did the believers at Jerusalem do what they did? Because this formidable practice was peculiar to the church at Jerusalem, it is probable that an outside force might have contributed to it. Remember that these disciples were all conversant with what Jesus had once said regarding the destruction of Jerusalem. The reason the disciples at Jerusalem did sell their properties, Hincks writes, was apparently to prevent those properties from being ruined by the upcoming destruction of Jerusalem foretold by the Lord Jesus Christ.[25]

Whatever might have been the cause, the custom of selling one's properties and submitting the proceeds for a common use was not practiced by Christians in general; a greater proportion of believers retained their properties but did maintain a fund, made up of weekly and monthly offerings, to take care of the poor in their midst.

The weekly and monthly contribution plan by the first Jewish Christians was commended by Apostle Paul. It continued for a period of time and was spoken of by Justin Martyr (100-165 A.D.), Tertullian (155-240 A.D.), and Cyprian (200-258 A.D.).

Justin Martyr's second apology records the following about the Church in his days:

> "Such as are wealthy, and are willing, every one freely contribute what they think fit, which is gathered together and deposited with the president, (i.e. the bishop), who out of it relieves orphans, widows, sick persons, prisoners, strangers, and all such as are in want." [26]

Regarding how church funds were raised, Tertullian puts it succinctly:

> "Whatsoever we have in the treasury of our churches is not raised by taxation, as though we put men to ransom their religion, but every man, once a month, or when it pleaseth him, bestoweth what he thinks proper – but not without he be willing, for no man is compelled, but left to his own free discretion: and that which is thus given is not bestowed in vanity, but in relieving the poor, and upon children destitute of parents, and in the maintenance of aged and feeble persons." [27]

It was for the sake of the Poor, Orphans, Widows, & Strangers (POWS) in the midst of the believers that Apostle Paul recommended that believers should make weekly and monthly donations whenever they gathered. [28] And we find in the writings of these early Christian writers that the churches were doing just that: they gave ONLY OFFERINGS to take care of the destitute and needy. They did not engage themselves in the old covenant practice of tithing for whatsoever reason.

---

[25] Hincks, *The Claims of the Clergy to Tithes and Other Church Revenues,* 14-15.
[26] Ibid., 15.
[27] Ibid.
[28] Ibid., 15-16.

Ministers of the Gospel Classified under 'the Poor'

Early preachers of the gospel were generally known to be materially poor and were seen to be among the poor class. In moving from one place to another, they counted on the hospitality of the hearers of their message for support. Likewise stationary ministers who had devoted themselves to the work of the ministry were also counted as part of the poor and supported from the offerings of the local church. These ministers accepted nothing more than the minimal support package they were provided with. Early ministers of the gospel "were made partakers with the poor and afflicted in the contributions of the church."[29] This was the beginning when ministers began to be paid by their local churches.

However, it should be noted that the early ministers were supported by their local churches only in cases where the former were unable to support themselves as a consequence of their ecclesiastical duties. This support scheme was extended to other clerical offices like the president, overseer, or bishop. Unfortunately this privilege became abused by the clergy. From this modest beginning of partaking with the poor, as having no other means of financial support, has arisen the wealth and grandeur of the clergy,[30] Hincks laments.

It appears from Cyprian's epistles that around 248 A.D. ministers in his time were also supported by their local churches. However, Cyprian noted that any minister who accepted such support must also resolve to lead a simple life,[31] not the materialistic-centered life we see portrayed today by a number of preachers worldwide. Cyprian also makes no mention of tithing as a church practice neither did he make any allusion of ministers receiving tithes. This is an indication that tithing was a non-event during the third century in the history of Christianity.

As late as the middle of the fifth century, Hincks writes, we have proof in the writings of Leo, bishop of Rome, that tithing had not existed in the church. Due to their personal interest, Hincks writes, "the clergy pressed much more earnestly the duty of giving to the church, but they had not yet ventured so far as to specify a quantity which they uniformly required."[32]

---

[29] Hincks, *The Claims of the Clergy to Tithes and Other Church Revenues*, 16.
[30] Ibid.
[31] Ibid.
[32] Ibid.

Bishops Authorized to Manage Church Funds

At an earlier period, the church began to receive donations of lands whose proceeds were intended to take care of the poor. Some churches became so wealthy and the funds were misappropriated by the clergy; they were not properly used for the poor. At the council of Antioch in 340 A.D., the bishops were authorized to manage the funds of the churches in their jurisdiction. It was stipulated that the bishops and the clergy under them should only take from the church coffers what was necessary for their daily upkeep. [33] However, this infringement did not stop the bishops and clergy from getting in the way of the portion of funds that was to be distributed to the poor.

Therefore, as we have just seen, church funds were solely made up of voluntary contributions from the brethren. The believers did not pay any tithes because they knew it was a Judaism-centered doctrine, which had been written off by their Lord and Savior, Jesus Christ, by nailing on the cross.

Regarding the form of financial contributions in the early church, Hincks writes,

> "So far as we have yet gone the funds of the churches arose out of voluntary contributions of no fixed amount, or donations of land, and were professedly intended for the assistance of the poor and afflicted, though the clergy had by this time come to be supported along with the poor from these funds, and, in consequence, demand for more liberal supply had become pressing." [34]

On how the believer of Christ today ought to give, Hiley Ward writes, "For the Christian who bears the name of a follower of his Savior, the beginning place continues always to be with Christ. Even in giving."[35] What Ward is highlighting here is that giving to the church must be a free and spontaneous response from the heart. The amount to be given must be decided by the giver, and not imposed by any third party.

---

[33] Hincks, *The Claims of the Clergy to Tithes and Other Church Revenues*, 17.
[34] Ibid.
[35] Wretlind, *Shekels, Dollars, and Sense*, 5-6.

THE IMPOSITION OF TITHING

TITHING: A FRAUDULENT CHARGE on GRACE

The institution of tithing in the Church is an issue that has been debated for several years. In the following pages we will show how tithing was usurped from its old covenant Jewish setting and introduced into the ecclesiastical system of worship in a gradual and systematic way.

As we have said before, church funds were made up of freewill offerings. As the clergy looked for avenues through which they could raise more money, they saw the old covenant law of tithing as a lucrative spot. However, that could not be served to the believers as plain as it was for fear of rejection. So, what they did was to use the "grace," which believers of Christ in general enjoy, as a net to catch their fish (tithe). They urged the members of their congregation to give to God as an appreciation for the grace God has given them. They urged them to give not less than what the Jews gave (10%) since the Jews did not enjoy the grace that followers of Christ enjoy. Consequently, the tithes were enforced as a divine obligation still binding on Christians, [36] Hincks laments.

When the clergy realized they had gotten their breakthrough, tithing gradually became established as a church doctrine, as Hincks testifies here-below:

---

[36] Hincks, *The Claims of the Clergy to Tithes and Other Church Revenues*, 17.

> "This was at first done cautiously and modestly, but as the submission of the people was experienced, a boldness was assumed which is truly astonishing, and for some time this new demand formed a chief subject of preaching."[37]

During this period, only those who were persuaded by the manipulative words of the clergy did pay tithes to them. Others who thought it was wrong refrained from any engagements. To put a seal on tithing as a measure to bring its non-adherents on board, church decrees were made, and the civil power was called in to enforce them, as Hincks tells us here-below:

> "For a long time the tithes were given only at the freewill of those who could be persuaded that it was right, - then church censures and canons were obtained, and at last the civil power was brought to enforce them."[38]

Casian the Hermit

We know from the account of Cassian the Hermit that the first account of tithes were paid by freewill to holy abbots in Egypt, and were meant to take care of the poor. Here-below is an expression of gratitude by Abbot John in the early fifth century following the collection of tithes, as reported by Cassian:

> "I gladly embrace this instance of your religious bounty, entrusted to my dispensation, for first fruits and tithes faithfully offered as charities to the poor are a sacrifice of sweet-smelling savour to the Lord."[39]

In the late fifth century, Eugippus, testifying from the life of Severinus, tells us that tithes were freely paid in Pannonia (a province of the Roman Empire, now the region comprising western Hungary, parts of Eastern Austria, and portions of Slovenia, Croatia, and Serbia). However, that happened following the persuasive influences of the clergy who claimed that the tithes were going to be used for the poor.[40]

There is an interesting story relating to tithing in the history of the Church that is worth mentioning here. Having suffered a bad harvest, the believers at Lauriacum (a town in Austria) declined the payment of tithes. The priests did employ their art of manipulation to coerce the believers into paying tithes by saying that if the latter paid their tithes punctually, they were not only going to receive eternal salvation, but

---

[37] Hincks, *The Claims of the Clergy to Tithes and Other Church Revenues, 17.*
[38] Ibid.
[39] Ibid., 18
[40] Ibid.

were also to enjoy the blessings of this life.[41] And this is the same manipulative strategy that most pastors are applying on the members of their congregation today to lure them into paying tithes.

Allocation of Church Funds in the 7th Century

By the seventh century, the church had begun setting apart particular portions of church funds reserved for specific purposes. In some churches, the funds were divided into three parts: one part went to the poor, the second and third parts went to the clergy, and to building and maintenance respectively. In other churches, the funds were divided into four equal parts distributed among the poor, the clergy, building and maintenance, and the fourth part went to the bishop. Sadly, a greater portion of the funds that was supposed to have been reserved for the poor was then alienated from them. [42]

France: New Churches Barred from Collecting Tithes

By 800 A.D., tithing had become an established doctrine in the Church to the extent that particular churches held claims to the right of tithes that had customarily been paid to them. As a consequence, in France, decrees were made forbidding new churches from receiving tithes that had traditionally been paid to older ones. [43]

Council of Lyons' Decree on Tithes

As the years passed by, Christians could choose to pay their tithes into churches or at lay monasteries. The payment of tithes into monasteries flourished over time because the Christians trusted that their tithes would not be misappropriated. However, the tithe, which was obtained for the benefit of the poor, Hincks writes, ended up being used in a great measure for the luxury and vices of monks and nuns. The preference of the monastery over the local church for the payment of tithes excited the jealousy of the clergy who pushed so hard for the creation of a canon at the council of Lyons in 1274 A.D. This canon stipulated that henceforth all tithes must be paid to the churches, not monasteries anymore. [44]

---

[41] Hincks, *The Claims of the Clergy to Tithes and Other Church Revenues, 18.*
[42] Ibid., 19.
[43] Ibid.
[44] Ibid., 20.

Tithe-Collection & the Clerical Lifestyle

Having the monopoly to collect tithes, the spending habit of the clergy suddenly escalated at the detriment of the poor, as Hincks tells us here-below:

> "...*but the expenditure of the priesthood went on increasing until the poor were entirely defrauded of their share in the church funds;* and at the suppression of the monasteries, all the property originally acquired by them for the use of the poor, and which, notwithstanding the desperate corruption of religious houses, had in some degree benefited them, being arbitrarily seized by the king for himself and his courtiers, the poor were left so totally unprovided for that poor laws shortly became necessary." [45]

To conclude, Hincks writes:

> "The history of tithes is a history of priestcraft and imposition; and it is an institution which is any thing but respectable or venerable from its antiquity, since it grew with the corruption of the church – was perfected in its worst times – and was established by those arts which have been its foulest disgrace." [46]

The clergy, for the sake of money, violated the New Covenant principle of Grace Alone (GRACE cannot be bought with money or supported by the Law) by enabling the believers to practice the law of tithing. William Hincks expatiates on this here-below:

> "Let me not be supposed to insinuate what I am sure would be most unjust, that the body of the clergy, or any large proportion of them, deliberately sacrificed known principles, or oppose what they believe to be good. Many of them may not be exactly the men who ought to be engaged in the christian ministry; and there may be more who disgrace it than there could be in a church not publicly endowed. But they are, generally speaking, estimable - often distinguished for their piety and benevolence – truly valuable ministers of the gospel, - and it is from their education, and the natural influence of their situation, that they derive that notorious political bias to which it is necessary we should advert, but which we charge as a fault, not on the individuals, but on the constitution of the church.
>
> It is for the public to consider whether it be for their advantage thus to provide a body of men, generally respectable from their character and education, and possessed of much influence from their situations, who are pre-disposed in favour of power, and against even the most beneficial changes, who have themselves well learned, and are ready to enforce the lesson of submission to authority, and all whose interests and sympathies are with the *few* against the *many*. If they do not expect advantage from *such* a body, let them set their faces against all public provision for a clergy, and leave the ministers of religion, as in the first ages of the Christian church, to be chosen by those whom they are to serve, and supported by the voluntary contributions of those who respect their virtues and value their labours." [47]

---

[45] Hincks, *The Claims of the Clergy to Tithes and Other Church Revenues*, 21.
[46] Ibid., 22.
[47] Ibid., 8.

In conclusion, Hincks writes:

> "If religion, and the blessings of religion, depend on an endowed clergy, all good men must unite in supporting their claims, and welcoming the inconveniences which cannot be separated from the system; but if it appear, not only that religion could subsist, but that the cause of pure and practical religion might be expected to flourish much more without them – that their establishment must be attended with injustice to persons of different religious opinions – and that their political influence is highly injurious to the public interests, then it is equally evident that good men, enlightened friends of religion, of justice, and of their country, must be opposed to all public provision for the clergy, and desirous of seeing the unhallowed connection between church and state finally dissolved.
>
> I leave these remarks on the general question of the expediency of a publicly endowed clergy, to the reader's consideration; only reminding him, in conclusion, that there may be such a body, if thought needful, without the tithe system, and without the corruptions of our present church establishment." [48]

If Christianity be what we take it to be: a religion given by God to bless mankind, William Hincks argues, then it must surely inspire men and women with a zeal that is sufficient enough to fund its projects. [49] The clergy must not, by their own power, implement measures in the Church, such as tithing, that are a betrayal of the very purpose for which the Church exists.

REASONS FOR THE IMPOSITION OF TITHING

1. Claims to the Divine Right of Tithes

One of the reasons that prompted the clergy to collect tithes from the believers in their various churches was the erroneous claim held by the clergy: some clergy believed that it was their divine right to have the tithes as servants of God. Some of the clergy and their partisans had even gone ahead to stage violent declarations calling forth for the institution of their 'imaginary rights.' [50] "Let their claims be temperately discussed and decided upon according to the principles of reason and justice, without malice and without prejudice," William Hincks writes. [51]

The divine right of tithes initiated by church leaders is founded on the connection, albeit unparalleled, of the Levitical priesthood of the Old Testament to:

---

[48] Hincks, *The Claims of the Clergy to Tithes and Other Church Revenues,* 8-9.
[49] Ibid., 6.
[50] Ibid., 3.
[51] Ibid.

(1) certain New Testament passages that call for the support of ministers of the Gospel, and

(2) the conclusion derived from the custom of paying tithes in certain occasions among some ancient nations: that God has, from the origin of creation, ordained that tithes be brought to Him, and given to His immediate servants. [52]

The New Testament passages in question include Matthew 10:9-10, Luke 10:7-8, 1 Corinthians 9:13-14, Galatians 6:6, and 1 Timothy 5:17-18. It should be remarked that none of these passages, and the entire New Testament, in general, authorizes the collection or payment of tithes in churches. These passages simply exhort believers to support the ministers of the gospel in their midst. We will state them here below and give a short commentary thereof:

Matthew 10:9-10

[9] "Don't take any money in your money belts - no gold, silver, or even copper coins.

[10] Don't carry a traveler's bag with a change of clothes and sandals or even a walking stick. Don't hesitate to accept hospitality, because those who work deserve to be fed."

Luke 10:7-8

[7] Don't move around from home to home. Stay in one place, eating and drinking what they provide. Don't hesitate to accept hospitality, because those who work deserve their pay.

[8] If you enter a town and it welcomes you, eat whatever is set before you.

1 Corinthians 9:13-15

[13] Don't you realize that those who work in the temple get their meals from the offerings brought to the temple? And those who serve at the altar get a share of the sacrificial offerings.

[14] In the same way, the Lord ordered that those who preach the Good News should be supported by those who benefit from it.

[15] Yet I have never used any of these rights. And I am not writing this to suggest that I want to start now. In fact, I would rather die than lose my right to boast about preaching without charge.

Galatians 6:6

[6] Those who are taught the word of God should provide for their teachers, sharing all good things with them.

1 Timothy 5:17-18

---

[52] Hincks, *The Claims of the Clergy to Tithes and Other Church Revenues*, 9.

17 Elders who do their work well should be respected and paid well, especially those who work hard at both preaching and teaching.

18 For the Scripture says, "You must not muzzle an ox to keep it from eating as it treads out the grain." And in another place, "Those who work deserve their pay!"

Our Commentary

As clearly shown, there is no place in the five passages of Scripture above where believers are called upon to set aside 10% of their income as support fund for those that labor in the ministry of preaching. The children of Israel, safe the Levites, were explicitly commanded by God to render 10% of their agricultural produce and cattle unto the Levites to be counted as the Levites' inheritance. If the Lord had wanted believers of Christ to set aside 10% of their income, and hand over the same to their pastor as the pastor's property or inheritance, or even as a support package for the ministry of the Church, then He would have said so explicitly in the Scripture. But that is not the case.

Apostle Paul: I'd Rather Die than Take from the Church

Note that in 1 Corinthians 9:15, Paul, as a minister of God, personally rejected the idea of him being supported by the offerings of the church, which he saw as a form of charge for the preaching of the gospel. Paul would prefer to die than see himself being supported from the offerings of a local church.

The stance taken by the Apostle to the Gentiles with respect to a minister's support should not be mistaken for a biblical law or rule. This is simply the apostle's will and determination. Based on the apostle's statement, one cannot make a general conclusion that a minister of the gospel cannot be supported from the offerings of their local church. Making such an inference would be ridiculous. This is because it is but normal that pastors, who do not have any job from which they can sustain themselves, or who cannot work outside the church due to a high demand of their clerical duties, be supported by the local church in which they serve. However, this condition must be decided by the local body of believers through its council of elders, and not in a singlehanded fashion by one man: the pastor of the local church institution.

That notwithstanding, when we critically look at those New Testament passages purported to validate the payment of the clergy, we will come to realize that they were not referring to payment of any kind per se but to that hospitality that the believers of the church ought to render to the preacher who journeys about from place to place to bless the church with the message of the gospel.

It is an incontestable fact that the ministry of any local church should be honorably supported in the present time; but, in the past, the bishops or overseers of local churches were persons who were able and willing to distribute of their abundance to the brethren than holding claim to any right to material assistance from the latter. It is remarkable to note that, Hincks writes, "There is manifestly nothing said in the New Testament of any payment to those who held offices in the churches." [53] With regards to tithes, Hincks cautions, "The New Testament then contains absolutely nothing in favour of tithes, nor of any right of the clergy to take from the people." [54]

"Those who work deserve their pay"

When the Lord, in Luke 10:7, said, "Those who work deserve their pay," the context in which that statement was uttered explains its meaning. Reading from verse one you will see that the Lord had sent, in pairs, seventy-two of his disciples to a number of towns. In verse four, he tells them not to take any money with them, a traveler's bag, nor an extra pair of sandals. In verse six, He says if the disciples are received by their hosts, then the blessing (i.e. Good News) will abide with the latter. And, finally, in verse seven, He tells the disciples not to hesitate to accept the hospitality offered them by the hosts because "those who work deserve their pay." We hope you now get the whole picture clearly. In a nutshell, the hospitality of the host is not a right of the preacher but a privilege.

Tithe: An Exclusive Levitical Right

The Levites in the old covenant had a right to tithes as their personal property because tithes were given to them in the first place "in exchange for the portion of land to which they had an equal right with the other tribes of the Israel, in a country which they all took possession of in concert, and which was directly and miraculously given by God to the whole nation: tithes, therefore, were not merely or chiefly the salary of an office, but a rightful share of divided

---

[53] Hincks, *The Claims of the Clergy to Tithes and Other Church Revenues*, 10.
[54] Ibid., 11.

property." [55]

Hincks went further to stress that due to their geopolitical situation, tithes did not constitute "the whole property of the Levites, but they had also cities appointed for their residence throughout the land, besides various valuable perquisites, belonging to the priests." [56]

Tithing in Judaism, Christianity: Two Distinct Contexts

This fact must be acknowledged: The government of the Hebrews and the context under which tithes were given are completely different from the government of the Church and the context in which the Church finds itself. Hincks elaborates on this issue here-below:

> "We should consider the peculiar nature of the Hebrew government: the land was considered as being bestowed on the nation by God: they were taught that it was his property in a peculiar sense, as being under his direct government, and he being their only king (though in their folly and disobedience they afterwards made a change in this respect): and as the land was freely given to them, being divided so that each man had his own property, subject only to a charge of a tenth for the support of a tribe of their brethren, who, instead of laboring on the soil, were employed in rendering other important services to the public, and were also, as it were, the appointed ministers of their sovereign, - they could have no possible ground of complaint; but to nations differently situated the matter must appear in a very different light." [57]

In the Scripture, the Lord God specifically commanded the non-Levitical tribes of Israel to give onto their Levite brethren a tithe of their cultivated crops and herds (that were from the land of Israel). If God also wanted the Church to tithe, He would have given that revelation in the Scripture, "but the Christian Scriptures," Hincks writes, "which alone we receive as containing such a revelation, make no demand of the kind, therefore no Divine law or religious obligation imposes on us this or any similar burden." [58]

2. The Boycott of State Support

A second reason that was put forward by the clergy as a justification for the collection of tithes was the boycott of State support. During a period of time, it should be recalled, the clergy were supported by the State. So, the clergy thought that if they were left to be supported by secular establishments, which do not serve the cause of religion, the

---

[55] Hincks, *The Claims of the Clergy to Tithes and Other Church Revenues*, 11.
[56] Ibid.
[57] Ibid., 12-13.
[58] Ibid., 14.

Church might come under the patronage of civil government. Where the clergy are not appointed by, and depended on those that they serve, there is no security that the service they render would be acceptable, they claimed. Where the Church is supported by the public expense, it is likely to be viewed as a mere arm of State policy. This would lead many to regard the Church with indifference or dislike, they concluded. The Church must reject any aids from the civil society, they reasoned, for Jesus said, "My kingdom is not of this world," and "Render unto Caesar the things which are Caesar's, and unto God the things which are God's," [59] they added. By implication, Christians were called upon to donate 10% of their income as tithe to support the clergy.

However, as convincing as this might sound, it might have been a façade or ploy to get the brethren submit a tenth of their possessions under the auspices of the clergy. Whenever the word of God is sacrificed on the platter of 'reason' or 'circumstance,' know there is a hidden agenda somewhere. On many counts the Bible is very explicit about this: tithing was for Judaism, not Christianity.

Therefore, it was the fear of losing their remuneration, and not the preservation of biblical truth, that pushed the clergy to demand the collection of tithes from the believers, as explained by Pastor William Hincks here-below:

> "As the plans proposed for the abolition of tithes have seldom gone farther than to substitute some other mode of payment for a peculiarly odious and mischievous tax, it might not seem requisite for us to enter on the question (which we cannot here treat as it deserves) of the expediency of having a publicly endowed clergy, did not the clerical advocates themselves appear to take it for granted that the loss of tithes must soon be followed by an entire loss of their revenues, and make the necessity of an endowed ministry a part of their case. They have, perhaps, not acted prudently, for the greater number have hitherto only objected to tithes as an injurious mode of taxation, and not a few even of those whose love of justice makes them wish to see different sects treated more equally, have thought of an extension of public favour to others, without its being withdrawn from the church, which now exclusively possesses it." [60]

Tithing in the Church: The Handwork of Men

Given that no single precept in the New Testament authorizes the collection or payment of tithes in the Church, the practice of tithing in the Church as a doctrine has simply been a well-crafted establishment by the clerical class, as explained by Hincks here-below:

---

[59] Hincks, *The Claims of the Clergy to Tithes and Other Church Revenues,* 5-6.
[60] Ibid., 4.

"It has been imposed by priestcraft on ignorance and superstition, and it is a great injury done to our holy religion when it is represented as patronizing such devices, - an injury, however, from which, in this enquiring age, we may hope to see it fully and finally delivered, since already the Divine right of tithes is a point which many of their defenders are ashamed to touch."[61]

THE ORIGIN OF TITHING IN USA

1873: Tithing First Suggested in USA

Hudnut-Beumier tells us that tithing was never preached nor practiced in the United States until 1873 when it was first suggested.[62] What prompted this drastic move is what we are going to look at in the following lines.

Tithing's Introduction Influenced by Hardship

Due to the hardship introduced by the Cold War in the 19th century, Hudnut-Beumier tells us that churches sought mechanisms through which they could raise funds. Antebellum writers were much concerned about convincing Christians to give. In his book, *The Apostolic Treasury in 1870*, Edward P. Gray, the Episcopal priest in Reconstruction era Minnesota, was concerned in detailing the cost factors of the church's finance. These were: the bishop's salary, clergyman's salary, parish expenses, parish school, parish charities, diocesan schools, diocesan missions, domestic missions, Indian missions, foreign missions, freedmen's commission, convention expenses, divinity school, aged and infirm clergy, orphan asylum, hospital, Prayer Book Society, Church Book Society, Tract Society and increase of the ministry. Gray's concern was how the church would be able to fund these projects. However, Gray believed that all church finances should come from freewill offerings, not tithes.[63]

Due to low salaries, William Crosswell Doane, the Episcopal bishop of Albany, New York, lamented the fact that just in his first eight months in office, he had made thirty-four changes in appointment out of the eighty-four priests in his care.[64]

It was for this reason, Hudnut-Beumier tells us, that the church leaders saw tithing as an attractive source of funding church projects. At this

---

[61] Hincks, *The Claims of the Clergy to Tithes and Other Church Revenues,* 14.
[62] James Hudnut-Beumier, *In Pursuit of the Almighty's Dollar: A History of Money and American Protestantism* (USA: University of North Carolina Press, 2007), 53.
[63] Ibid., 48.
[64] Hudnut-Beumier, *In Pursuit of the Almighty's Dollar,* 49.

time, the church was no more prepared to accept from its members anything short of ten percent. [65]

Church leaders see tithing as a lucrative spot for raising funds. They care less of the soundness of the gospel message. Their interest is how they can squeeze 10% worth of income off their members' pockets. Some of these pastors are even bold to say that if they do not collect tithes, they can't do ministry properly. Unlike Christ, they have reduced the gospel into monetary terms. Unlike Christ, money has become the priory over the truth of the gospel. Regarding this misplacement of priority, Wells writes, "You may have already been caught with the wrong priorities if the church finances are your first concern over the truth and deliverance for God's people." [66]

A book published in 1878 entitled *The Christian Treasury* by C. P. Jennings chronicled tithing as a potential source for financing church projects. Jennings, dean of the St. Andrew's Cathedral, Syracuse, New York, argued that the "tythe" was the only acceptable form of sustenance for the church and its ministers. A voluntary Old Testament tithe, Jennings continues, was biblical and still binding on Christians. [67]

"It would be a great mistake," Rolston laments, "for Christians leaders to think that they can solve the problems of Christian stewardship today simply by an intensified emphasis on tithing." "Christian stewardship," he continues, "must go much deeper and have a broader basis than the Old Testament law of the tithe." [68]

1890: Tithing Finally Established in USA

By 1890, tithing had become an established ritual in the United States whereby parishioners would present their "tithes and offerings" to the Lord, which was followed by the singing of the doxology recognizing that the presented tithes and offerings came from God. [69]

Therefore, it was the fundraising desire that motivated church leaders to excavate the old covenant law of tithing from the cross of Christ, where it had been nailed, revived it, and exacted members of their congregation to practice it through manipulative preaching. The laws, including tithing, circumcision, and a host of others, which were against us, have been nailed to the cross of Christ more than two

---

[65] Hudnut-Beumier, *In Pursuit of the Almighty's Dollar*, 51.
[66] Wells, *The Great Tithing Debate*, 1.
[67] Hudnut-Beumier, *In Pursuit of the Almighty's Dollar*, 51.
[68] Wretlind, *Shekels, Dollars, and Sense*, 3.
[69] Hudnut-Beumier, *In Pursuit of the Almighty's Dollar*, 55-56.

thousand years ago. However, church leaders, to quote Wells, "simply refuse to let them die, especially the ones in Malachi." [70]

Zwingli's Contradiction on Tithing

Consider Ulrich Zwingli (1484-1531), the leader of the Reformation in Switzerland, whose view on tithing was that as tithes were not of divine authority in the new covenant, their payment should not be obligatory. [71] This was Zwingli's stance in 1519. However, in June 1523, after six churches from the countryside were in need of financial assistance from Zurich, Zwingli moderated his position on tithing and said that most forms of tithing were valid. [72] Zwingli's new view became that "even though tithing was not a divine right, it was a human right." So, for the sake of raising money, Zwingli had to make a compromise. And such is the same phenomenon with most ministers of the gospel today regarding the issue of tithes.

MINISTERS WHO DENOUNCED TITHING

A. THE REFORMATION PERIOD

Due to the fact that the New Testament does not support tithing in the Church, the Anabaptists, and especially the Swiss Anabaptists, in 1525, condemned in a radical manner the practice and abuse of tithing, calling for its abolition. [73]

1. Ainsworth & Johnson

The Separatists in Amsterdam, notably Ainsworth and Johnson, affirmed that as a religious law tithing was not binding on Christians. In Article 7 of their address to King James I of England in 1602-1603, the Separatists argued that ministers of the gospel should be supported from freewill offerings, not from the Jewish tithes and offerings. [74] Ainsworth and Johnson provided seven arguments against the continuation of tithing in the New Testament era. One of these was that the law of tithing came to a perpetual end with the change of the Levitical Priesthood, as recorded in Hebrews 7:12. While God gave tithes, first fruits, and other offerings to his priests, Ainsworth argued,

---

[70] Wells, *The Great Tithing Debate*, 6.
[71] Croteau, *You Mean I Don't Have to Tithe?* 29.
[72] Ibid.
[73] Ibid., 30.
[74] Ibid., 33.

Christ gave none of these to his priests. [75]

Note that one of the reasons why the Levitical Priesthood system was created was to appease the wrath of God through offerings and sacrifices (Leviticus 9:7). The priests presented these offerings and sacrifices before God in the Holy of Holies to cleanse the Israelites of their sins so they could draw closer to God. It was a custom that a tithe of the firstling was usually removed from the whole and handed to the priest.

Even though these offerings were presented to God, they did not appease God's wrath satisfactorily until Christ came. God's wrath was finally and satisfactorily appeased when Christ gave Himself up on the cross. It was for this reason that the baton of the Priesthood was immediately passed from Aaron to Jesus Christ. Since Jesus finally achieved what followers of Moses were striving to achieve through offerings (*offering* here does not refer to the usual freewill offerings that are given during church attendance) and sacrifices in the days of old, the followers of Jesus, therefore, have no reasons whatsoever to offer these stuffs in order to draw closer to God. All they need is to embrace, through faith, the One who did this on their behalf. And this will be counted onto them as righteousness. Anything beyond this is making mockery of the finished work of Christ on the cross.

2. John Smyth (1609)

John Smyth, a Separatist credited to be the first Baptist, arguing in the same line as Ainsworth said that a change in the Priesthood engendered a change in the Law, and since tithes were a part of the Law, believers under the new covenant were not bound to tithing because Christ, their High Priest, had set them free from that yoke. [76]

3. John Robinson (1610)

John Robinson, the pastor of the "Pilgrim Fathers" who supported the views of Ainsworth and Smyth on tithing, argued that, with respect to ordinances, the Law is abolished by the gospel in the same way the old covenant is abolished by the new. And because tithing was a part of the Law, it has been abolished by the gospel. Robinson also held the view that financial support for ministers of the gospel should come from voluntary offerings since tithing is no longer a valid practice for

---

[75] Croteau, *You Mean I Don't Have to Tithe? 33.*
[76] Ibid., 34.

the Church. [77]

Therefore, apart from John Calvin, whose view on tithing is ambiguous, and Zwingli, who later supported some form of tithing due to financial pressure, none of the reformers explicitly advocated tithing. [78] Basing their judgment on the Scripture, they found no reasons why the Church today should practice this old covenant religious law that was given to the Jews.

B.   POST REFORMATION ERA (1648 - 1873)

1.   Francis Turretin (1623-1687)

One of the first voices to have been heard during the Post Reformation tithing debate of the early 1870s was Francis Turretin, pastor at a church in Geneva and professor of Theology. Turretin affirmed that Christians are not bound by certain laws of the Old Testament such as tithing and first fruits. He added that the support for the pastor should come from voluntary contributions. [79]

2.   John Wesley (1703-1791)

John Wesley was an advocate of tithing. In his sermon on the three uses of money, John Wesley, the father of Methodism, said: earn all you can, save all you can, and give all you can. [80] Wesley advocated tithing, claiming it was a rule of Christian prudence. [81] Therefore, Wesley argued that Christians should not be confined to a particular percentage like the Jews, but that they should give all they can. "Render unto God," he continued, "not a tenth, not a third, not half, but all that is God's, be it more or less." [82]

As far as Wesley was concerned, tithing was mandatory for Christians. Wesley did not just advocate the payment of the usual portion of the tithes as found in the old covenant, but he went further to demand that believers pay a higher than ten percent. Tithe, according to Wesley, was a very weak offering if it ended at ten percent. [83]

---

[77] Croteau, *You Mean I Don't Have to Tithe? 34.*
[78] Ibid., 35.
[79] Ibid.
[80] Ibid., 35-36.
[81] Ibid., 36.
[82] Ibid
[83] Ibid.

RESISTANCE TO TITHING IN ENGLAND

Selden: Tithing is a Human Appointment

From the thirteenth century throughout the sixteenth century there had been a resistance to tithing in England. The resistance got to its peak in the seventeenth century with the introduction of Selden's publication in 1618 entitled *A History of Tithes.* In this book, Selden demonstrated that the practice of tithing under the new covenant was not a divine requirement, but a human appointment. [84]

Selden Forced to Recant His Tithing View

After having made this remark, Selden was summoned and threatened by a council. For fear of the unknown, Selden signed a document of recantation before the council where he stated that he was in error in his book on tithing. [85] Selden's book exposed the exactions of the clergy. So, the clergy did their best to force him to recant his outstanding statement on tithes so that their wells of such clandestine contributions should keep on flowing unperturbed.

1649: The English Parliament's Attempt to Abolish Tithes

Coming into terms that tithes were not of divine right, the English parliament, in 1649, passed a law ordering the abolition of tithes as soon as another plan to take care of the clergy could be agreed upon. [86] Different proposals were made for the maintenance of the clergy. One of such proposals was that the clergy be paid directly by the congregation.

The Worcester Petition

A group of ministers, who felt threatened by the news of the ongoing deliberations at the English parliament that were centered on abolishing the practice of tithing in English churches immediately came together and drafted the Worcester Petition. This petition made a bold declaration that the ministers of the gospel had the divine right of possessing the tithes. [87] Filled with a cloud of despair regarding their socio-economic status if there were no tithes, these ministers had no

---

[84] Croteau, *You Mean I Don't Have to Tithe?* 37.
[85] Ibid.
[86] Ibid.
[87] Ibid., 38.

choice but to do what they were not required by the Scripture to do. Nowhere does the Bible affirm tithes to be the property of ministers of the gospel under the new covenant.

Though the members of the English parliament were convinced that tithing had already been abolished by Christ's death on the cross, they did not proceed to legitimize the abolition of tithing in English churches due to the fact that there was no agreed maintenance plan for the clergy. So, the matter was dropped till further notice. [88]

Four years later, in 1653, the Little Parliament, led by Cromwell and the Independent Churches, concluded that tithing as a means of church fund-raising ought to be nullified since there were no biblical grounds for the continuation of such practice in the New Testament Church. Neither did Cromwell, the Little Parliament nor the Independent Churches view tithing as an eternal law, but as the best solution to the maintenance of the clergy. [89]

The Quakers

There were a number of pressure groups in England that stood up to resist the practice of tithing in the seventeenth century in that country. One of such groups was The Quakers. This group distributed its first tract in which it enumerated a number of reasons why tithing should be banned in the Church. The forwarded reasons included: [90]

(1) that tithes were only applicable to the Mosaic law and the Levites;

(2) that tithes were a ceremonial practice, and, consequently, have been abolished by the new covenant;

(3) that the support of ministers of the gospel should come from a voluntary, and not a mandatory, giving;

(4) that the New Testament nowhere supports the practice of tithing among the Body of Christ; and

(5) that the tithing system was only recently introduced into churches.

In response, an English Prelate tendered the following reasons why

---

[88] Croteau, *You Mean I Don't Have to Tithe? 38.*
[89] Ibid.
[90] Ibid., 39.

tithing should be practiced. These were: [91]

(1) that tithing existed prior to the Mosaic Law;

(2) that Christ has an equal right to tithes as Melchizedek;

(3) that Christ rebuked those that did not support ministers of the gospel; and

(4) that Christ commanded Christians to render unto Caesar what is Caesar's.

Gough made a rejoinder to the prelate's remarks in which he affirmed the following: [92]

(1) that the command to tithe is given nowhere in the Bible apart from the Levitical law;

(2) that Christ rebuked those who did not follow the teachings of his disciples, and not those who did not support them financially; and

(3) that the Quakers were not bound to obey the civil authorities in the event whereby the latter do compromise God's Word.

The Quakers were so firm in their resolve that they would expel from their group any member who paid tithes. Unfortunately, and sad to say, most of them were thrown into jails for refusing to tithe. However, by 1835 the Quakers were free from any further prosecution linked to their biblical stance on tithes. [93]

The English Baptists

The English Baptists were another group that wrestled with the tithing practice. In England, many of the early Baptists around 1656 decided to pay tithes into their churches not because it was a biblical practice but because they were obeying a civil law that rendered the payment of tithes to the church equivalent to the payment of taxes to the civil government. [94] Several other Baptist churches rejected the idea of tithes collection for the support of the clergy on the ground

---

[91] Croteau, *You Mean I Don't Have to Tithe? 39.*
[92] Ibid.
[93] Ibid.
[94] Ibid.

that tithing was an old covenant ordinance, which is totally inappropriate for the New Testament Church. [95]

With respect to tithing, the early Baptists found themselves in a very tight corner. On the one hand, they had embraced the fact that tithing was not a part of Christian doctrine and had resolved not to initiate it in their worship service. On the other hand, they did not want to disobey the civil law, which might have led them lose one or more religious freedom. These early Baptists were overwhelmed by two main controversies. The first was whether ministers of the gospel should be given a financial compensation for their service in the Body of Christ. Note that here tithing was out of place as a source of the financial compensation in question. The second was whether leaders of the Baptist church should accept tithes from the government for their income. [96] They came to the following conclusions: [97]

(1) that ministers of the gospel should be supported by their congregation;

(2) that these ministers must serve the gospel faithfully, and without greed; and

(3) that any minister who accepts tithes from any member of the congregation should be properly sanctioned according to Matthew 18:15-17. That is, they should be enlisted on the discipline roll of the church, and, if possible, excommunicated if they do not repent.

J. C. Philpot

The tithing issue had forced J. C. Philpot in 1835 to quit the Church of England and become a Particular Baptist. In his resignation letter, Philpot lamented why the clergy were paid from tithes. Philpot vehemently argued that the only New Testament authorized way of supporting ministers of the gospel was through the collection of freewill offerings. [98]

John MacDuff

John MacDuff was an English Presbyterian who spoke against the

---

[95] Croteau, *You Mean I Don't Have to Tithe?* 39.
[96] Ibid., 40.
[97] Ibid.
[98] Ibid., 42.

binding nature of tithes. MacDuff, in 1878, stressed that "the proportion of giving is left to an enlightened conscience." [99] He denounced any giving that is motivated by impulse or emotion.

The Tithe Act of 1936

Therefore, as we have seen here above, the practice of tithing by churches in England was, in the past, met by a strong resistance from groups that advocated spiritual renewal and radical discipleship. The resistance continued for hundreds of years before tithes were finally abolished in England by the Tithe Act of 1936. [100]

The Tithing Renewal (1873-Present Day)

Prior to 1873, none of the churches in North America had a tithing system to take care of the clergy. In the eighteenth century, support for the clergy came from taxes. Members of various church groups, such as the Baptists, Presbyterians, Quakers, and Episcopalians, were allowed to pay these taxes to their own clergy. In addition, funds were also raised by renting pews to families by rank. [101]

Mandatory Contributions Annulled in Connecticut and Massachusetts

However, in Connecticut (1818) and Massachusetts (1834), the mandatory requirement for the support of ministers of the gospel through taxes was gotten rid of in favour of voluntary contributions. This happened as a result of the Church and State having parted ways from each other. [102]

Clergy vs. Laity: Easing the Establishment of Tithing

Please remember this: in the Church Age, every Christian is a "priest," however, in the new covenant sense of the word. Tithing cannot exist in a "kingdom of priests." It can only exist in a system where there are non-priests (who bring the tithes) and priests (who collect the tithes and perform a ritual). It was not until the Church was differentiated into the clergy (the priestly group) and the laity (the commoners) that tithing was fraudulently introduced as a Church doctrine.

---

[99] Croteau, *You Mean I Don't Have to Tithe?* 42.
[100] Ibid., 46.
[101] Ibid., 49.
[102] Ibid.

Regarding this issue, Kelly writes:

> "The earliest church fathers and church historians gave ample evidence that there was no distinction between the laity and clergy for almost two hundred years. When this non-distinction was lost, when the clergy evolved into a superior hierarchy, when the local bishop was transformed into a 'bishop-priest,' when the doctrine of the priesthood of believers was pushed out of the way – then a full-time paid clergy began to emerge in church history, which opened the way for tithing to re-enter much later in support of an unscriptural exclusive 'priesthood' in the church. Unfortunately even most Protestant churches treat their preachers and pastors as 'priests' by expecting them to perform most of the priestly functions for the laity."[103]

---

[103] Russell Earl Kelly, *Should the Church Teach Tithing? A Theologian's Conclusions about A Taboo Doctrine* (USA: Writers Club Press, 2007), 180.

5

THE TITHE OF ABRAM
THE TITHE OF JACOB

Two references to tithing in the Old Testament that occurred prior to the Law of Moses have fueled anxiety on the debate regarding the legitimacy of tithing in the New Testament Church. Advocates for tithing in the church have argued that tithing must be a universal command since it was practiced by Abram and Jacob.

Most pro-tithe pastors have used the cases of Abram and Jacob as two examples of tithing to teach that tithing is a revelation from God. "How did Abraham and Jacob know about tithing when the law of tithing was given to Moses some 400 years later?" they argue. "The LORD must have revealed this mystery to them," they claim.

It is worthwhile to note that before the law of tithing was given to Moses on Mount Sinai, tithing had been practiced by a number of nations in the ancient world. It was a custom for tithes to be paid from war booty, as Hiley Ward (quoted from Wretlind) tells us here-below:

> "Tithing may be traced to the very beginnings of history. Egyptians tithed. About 3,000 B.C., Egyptians were giving one-tenth of their spoils of war to their gods.... The custom of giving a tenth to the gods of the ancient world is found also in Babylonia, Arabia, Greece, Rome, and China."[104]

Based on the fact that tithing was an ancient practice known to Abram and his grandson, Jacob, it is unlikely that the display of the knowledge of tithing as demonstrated by these two patriarchs was a

---

[104] Wretlind, *Shekels, Dollars, and Sense*, 10.

personal revelation from God. The Bible itself makes no claim that either of these men did possess any special revelation on tithing. Note that tithe is mentioned just once in the Bible in connection to Abram and Jacob. Secondly, while Abram tithed on the spoils he got from war, Jacob's tithe was merely a promise to God. He vowed to give God a tenth if the LORD would bless him. Did he actually fulfill his vow? We do not know from the Scripture.

In this chapter, we are going to study the tithe-related cases of Abram and Jacob to see whether they are justifiable grounds for the practice of tithing in the New Testament Church.

1. THE TITHE OF ABRAM

Genesis 14:13-24

[13] A man who had escaped came and reported this to Abram the Hebrew. Now Abram was living near the great trees of Mamre the Amorite, a brother of Eshkol and Aner, all of whom were allied with Abram.

[14] When Abram heard that his relative had been taken captive, he called out the 318 trained men born in his household and went in pursuit as far as Dan.

[15] During the night Abram divided his men to attack them and he routed them, pursuing them as far as Hobah, north of Damascus.

[16] He recovered all the goods and brought back his relative Lot and his possessions, together with the women and the other people.

[17] After Abram returned from defeating Kedorlaomer and the kings allied with him, the king of Sodom came out to meet him in the Valley of Shaveh (that is, the King's Valley).

[18] Then Melchizedek king of Salem brought out bread and wine. He was priest of God Most High,

[19] and he blessed Abram, saying, "Blessed be Abram by God Most High, Creator of heaven and earth.

[20] And praise be to God Most High, who delivered your enemies into your hand." Then Abram gave him a tenth of everything.

[21] The king of Sodom said to Abram, "Give me the people and keep the goods for yourself."

[22] But Abram said to the king of Sodom, "With raised hand I have sworn an oath to the LORD, God Most High, Creator of heaven and earth,

[23] that I will accept nothing belonging to you, not even a thread or the strap of a sandal, so that you will never be able to say, 'I made Abram rich.'

[24] I will accept nothing but what my men have eaten and the share that belongs to the men who went with me—to Aner, Eshkol and Mamre. Let them have their share."

ANALYSIS:

Point 1 (Genesis 14:20):

> ✓ **The Passage Justifies <u>an act</u>, not <u>the practice</u> of Tithing**

Genesis 14 is the place where *tithe*, not tithing, is first mentioned in the Bible. There is a distinction between the two terms. We refer to Abram's gesture in Genesis 14:20 as *tithe* and not *tithing* because while the latter is a customary practice, the former is merely an act. The payment of tithe by Abram to Melchizedek was a singular event. Apart from this one-time Abram-Melchizedek event, there is no other place in the Scripture that provides us with any records of Abram paying tithes to anyone else. This is an indication that Abram did not likely practice tithing as a divine commandment as did his progeny, the children of Israel. Scripturally-speaking, to add, the practice of tithing, as an expressed ordinance, was never associated with Abram.

Point 2 (Genesis 14: 20):

> ✓ **It was 'Abram,' <u>not Abraham</u>, who paid tithes to**

The second point to note here is that the tithes were given by *Abram* ("high father"), and *not Abraham* ("father of a multitude"). Abram became *"Abraham"* only later on in Genesis 17:5.

Genesis 17:5

[5] No longer will you be called Abram; your name will be Abraham, for I have made you a father of many nations.

This is very significant in counteracting the establishment of tithing in the Church that is based on a false extrapolation of the tithe of Abram. By faith, followers of Christ are the children of Abraham, "the father of a multitude," not Abram. Since the tithes were not paid by Abraham, through whom followers of Christ are connected by faith, there is, therefore, no obligation for the latter to pay tithes to whomsoever or practice the same as a custom.

Point 3 (Genesis 14:18-20):

> ✓ **The Object of Abram's Tithe, a Paradoxical Figure**

Thirdly, Abram's tithe was given benevolently to a mysterious figure,

Melchizedek, who at the same time was paradoxical in connection to his collection of tithes and him being likened to Christ. Who really was Melchizedek? The answer to this question is as numerous as the number of theologians who discuss it. The impossibility to trace the historical genealogy of Melchizedek poses the following fundamental problem: "To whom were tithes to be offered following the disappearance of Melchizedek?" (Note that there was no organized cult for Melchizedek's pronouncement of blessings on Abram).

Abram-Melchizedek Encounter: Not a Justification for Tithing

Hebrews 7:1-3 below sheds some light on the personality of Melchizedek.

Hebrews 7:1-3

[1] This Melchizedek was king of Salem and priest of God Most High. He met Abraham returning from the defeat of the kings and blessed him,

[2] and Abraham gave him a tenth of everything. First, the name Melchizedek means "king of righteousness"; then also, "king of Salem" means "king of peace."

[3] Without father or mother, without genealogy, without beginning of days or end of life, resembling the Son of God, he remains a priest forever.

Many pro-tithe ministers have held the claim that since Jesus, in the person of Melchizedek, received tithes from Abram, Christians should pay tithes to Jesus through his appointed servants, the leaders of local churches. It is true that the description of Melchizedek in Hebrews 7 above indicates he was an apparition of Jesus Christ. Yet that does not form any sound basis for the formulation of a Christian doctrine of tithing for numerous reasons, which are discussed in this book.

If Melchizedek, whom Hebrews 7 reveals to be Jesus Christ, collected a tithe from Abram prior to the Law and new covenant, and if after more than fifteen hundred years following the Melchizedek-Abram encounter Jesus did not collect or teach his followers to tithe but assured them that he had fulfilled the whole Law by his death on the cross, it means that Jesus (or the Christ-like Melchizedek, going by the revelation of Hebrews 7), does not commend tithing as a doctrine for the New Testament Church.

Point 4 (Genesis 14: 20):

> ✓ **The Tithe of Abram was not a Command/Obligation**

Fourthly, since this incident in Abram's life preceded the Mosaic Law by over four hundred years, Abram's act of giving a tithe to Melchizedek was not imposed upon him. This justifies the fact that prior to the Mosaic Law tithing was not an obligation or a divine commandment. And since that was the case, this passage cannot be taken to be a justification for tithing for generations after Abram. Therefore, church leaders who quote this passage as a biblical basis for tithing are being theologically dishonest to themselves. We know, of course, that they do this simply for the purpose of getting 10% of the hard-earned income of members of their congregation.

Abram's Tithe Different from the Commanded Tithe

The tithe of Abram, it should be noted, was completely different from the one the Jews were commanded to give. First, while Abram gave a tithe to Melchizedek, the Jews gave tithes to the Levites. Second, unlike the Jews, who were commanded to give tithes to the Levites, Abram's tithe was never commanded by Melchizedek, neither was it commanded by his God, YAHWEH.

Point 5 (Genesis 14:14-20):

✓ **Abram's tithe came from the Spoils of War**

It is important to note that the tithe that Abram gave to Melchizedek did not come from Abram's personal property. It came from the spoils of war. If the Church should preach that members of their congregation should pay tithes, basing their judgment on Abram's example, as recorded in this passage, then, in order to collect tithes from their members, the Church must be ready to tell the former to do what Abram did: fight, win a war, and bring a tithe of the gains and drop it into the tithe basket of the church.

The Payment of Tithes: An Ancient Custom

Instances of tithing among the Romans, Greeks, and other ancient nations revealed that tithes were usually paid from the spoils of war or from goods and properties given on special occasions.[105] This might have probably accounted for Abram's act of tithing to Melchizedek. Given that tithing was an ancient custom, it is most likely that Moses adopted the tithing plan rather than originated it, William Hincks

---

[105] Hincks, *The Claims of the Clergy to Tithes and Other Church Revenues*, 14.

affirms. [106]

Point 6 (Genesis 14:21-24):

> ✓ **Abram returned the 90% of War Booty in his Keeping**

After giving a tithe to Melchizedek, Abram returned the remaining 90% of the war booty to the king of Sodom following his vow in Genesis 14:22-24. Therefore, Abram gave up 100%, not 10%.

Point 7 (Genesis 14:22-24):

> ✓ **The story demonstrates Abram's *Integrity*, <u>Not Tithing</u>**

As a principle of interpreting any biblical account, we must remember that the climax of a narrative is at the end, not at the beginning or middle, of the story.

On this issue, Kaiser and Silva write:

> "Narrative in its broadest sense is an account of specific space-time events and participants whose stories are recorded with beginnings, middles and ends....Readers too often project some moral or spiritual truth over a biblical character or event, paying more attention to the moral lesson they see in the narrative than to the story itself. *The underlying objection to interpreting the Bible in a moralistic, exemplary fashion for every narrative passage is that it destroys the unity of the message of the Bible.*"[107]

Also worthy to note is that a good interpretation of a biblical passage should not stand on inferences. The passage in question should be able to explain itself clearly to its audience without the aid of a theoretical construct.

The moral of Genesis 14 above, whose climax gravitates toward the end, was to demonstrate *Abram's integrity*. Abram chose not to possess what was not truly his own even though it was his legal right to make use of them by virtue of his victory in war. This is what the passage teaches. And this is what we, believers of Christ, should emulate.

---

[106] Hincks, *The Claims of the Clergy to Tithes and Other Church Revenues*, 14.
[107] Quoted from Kelly, *Should the Church Teach Tithing*, 14.

2. THE TITHE OF JACOB

Now, we will look at the so-called tithe of Jacob to ascertain whether it is a justifiable ground for the tithing doctrine in churches. Let's visit the biblical passage straightaway:

Genesis 28:20-22

20 Then Jacob made a vow, saying, "If God will be with me and will watch over me on this journey I am taking and will give me food to eat and clothes to wear

21 so that I return safely to my father's household, then the LORD will be my God

22 and this stone that I have set up as a pillar will be God's house, and of all that you give me I will give you a tenth."

Biblical Analysis

Point 1 (Genesis 28:20):

✓   Jacob made a vow

Genesis 28:20 opens with "And Jacob vowed a vow..." This is a clear indication that whatever portion of blessings Jacob will be giving to God is simply a promise from Jacob. The vow made by Jacob is exclusively Jacob's will; the content of the vow is decided by Jacob, not God. Even though Jacob was under no obligation to make the vow, he chose to do it for his own personal interest.

What Jacob has vowed to give to God cannot be qualified as a "biblical tithe" as defined by the Law of Moses. The reason is that the biblical tithe, which the children of Israel were to bring to God every year, was not to be initiated through a vow but by obedience to a divine command.

Point 2 (Genesis 28:20-21):

✓   Jacob's tithe was a conditional promise

What Jacob had promised to give to God was tied to a condition, which God would have to fulfil for Jacob's vow to be binding on Jacob. In other words, Jacob would render his vow to God if God does the following three things:

1. God be with him and guide him in his journey.

2. God provides him with bread to eat during the course of his journey.

3. God provides him with clothes to wear during the said journey.

And the execution of the three premises above must bring into effect the following for the vow to be totally binding on both parties:

4. That Jacob comes again to the house of his father, Isaac, in peace.

Point 3 (Genesis 28:22):

✓ Jacob vowed a tenth

Jacob finally revealed the content of his vow (28:22): "…and of all that thou shalt give me I will surely give the tenth unto thee." Jacob promises to give God a tenth. However, the Bible does not tell us whether the tenth was actually given or not. But let us assume it was given. Even with this assumption, the tenth of Jacob cannot be equated with the tithe given by the Jews, which was a divine command enshrined in the Law of Moses. Jacob's vow did not commit his progeny or the followers of Christ in anyway. It was a personal initiative, which, as will be explained below, was uncalled for. On the other hand, the tithe that the Jews gave to God was an initiative from God. It was a divine command, which was to be practiced by the children of Israel under the old covenant for the benefit of the entire nation.

Point 4 (Genesis 28:21):

✓ Jacob was sceptical about God's providence

Jacob declares that if God does points 1 to 3 above so that point 4 is achieved, then the Lord will be his God. This indicates that Jacob was somehow skeptical about God's guidance and provision over his life during the course of his adventurous trip. Jacob promised to be loyal to God if God brings to pass Jacob's heart desire.

The condition imposed by Jacob here brings into question Jacob's faith in God. Faith does not impose; faith believes irrespective of the odds. Remember that God had assured Jacob in Genesis 28:15 that He would be with Jacob and that He was going to bring into fulfillment everything He had spoken concerning Jacob without requesting any sacrifice from Jacob:

Genesis 28:15

¹⁵ I am with you and will watch over you wherever you go, and I will bring you back to this land. I will not leave you until I have done what I have promised you."

The fact that Jacob did not yield to God's words but went ahead to make an offer reveals Jacob's pessimism. Remember also what Jesus had told Thomas in John 20:29, "Thomas, because thou hast seen me, thou hast believed: blessed are they that have not seen, and yet have believed." As children of God of the new covenant, we are called upon simply to believe the words of God spoken through His Son, Jesus Christ, and through His prophets. We are not to make any vows to God to cause God to act on His promises. God is not a man that He should lie; He will bring to pass whatever promises He has spoken to us (Numbers 23:19).

Jacob likewise promised to make of the stone he had set up to be God's temple. The promises made by Jacob in a time of uncertainty reveal Jacob's lack of unflinching trust in God. He didn't believe God adequately enough to count on Him without having to persuade God by making the promises he made.

Why Was Jacob Skeptical?

We will need to look briefly at the reason for Jacob's skepticism. When Jacob was sent by his father, Isaac, to look for a wife in Padanaram, (Genesis 28:6-7), Jacob, moving toward Haran, came to a certain place where he dwelled there all night. As he lay down to sleep, the Lord God appeared to Jacob in a dream where He promised Jacob that He was going to give to Jacob and his descendants the land upon which Jacob was lying. This was mind-blowing to Jacob. It was unimaginable. It was this state of mind that pushed Jacob to make a vow to God even though God didn't require such.

Genesis 28:10-14

¹⁰ Jacob left Beersheba and set out for Harran.

¹¹ When he reached a certain place, he stopped for the night because the sun had set. Taking one of the stones there, he put it under his head and lay down to sleep.

¹² He had a dream in which he saw a stairway resting on the earth, with its top reaching to heaven, and the angels of God were ascending and descending on it.

¹³ There above it stood the LORD, and he said: "I am the LORD, the God of your

father Abraham and the God of Isaac. I will give you and your descendants the land on which you are lying.

14 Your descendants will be like the dust of the earth, and you will spread out to the west and to the east, to the north and to the south. All peoples on earth will be blessed through you and your offspring.

Putting ourselves in Jacob's shoes, and taking into consideration the limited exposure Jacob had with respect to the knowledge of God as expressed in the Scripture, we would probably act in the same way, or, perhaps, worse than Jacob did.

The Stakes: If God Does Not Respond

Jacob's imposed promises imply the following in the event whereby God does not respond to Jacob's request:

1. The clause "then shall the Lord be my God" will become redundant (28:21). By implication, the incremental fraction of Jacob's devotion to God if God had granted his request would be lost.

2. In addition, the stone Jacob had set for a pillar may not become a permanent place of worship (28:22).

3. Lastly, the vow of "a tenth" will not be given to God since there are no blessings from which to pay the vow (28:22).

6

TITHING: A SECULAR CUSTOM

TITHING: A CUSTOMARY PRACTICE IN THE ANCIENT NEAR EAST

"Giving a tithe (a portion) was not just a practice by Israel, in ancient history it was practiced throughout the Middle East. It was income for the king and his kingdom, like a tax. It may be regular, voluntary or prescribed by law of a certain country" [108]

We should be reminded that prior to the Law of Moses, tithing was a customary practice across several nations in the ancient Near East including Israel. There is, however, limited evidence in the Bible regarding the custom of tithe-giving in Israel. The Bible mentions only two cases (Abram's and Jacob's respectively), which we have just dealt with here-above.

To understand that tithing had been a customary form of taxation in ancient societies, we shall consider Egypt to be our case study. Most kings charged 10% (or a slightly different amount) as land tax from their residents given that the king was normally seen to be the natural owner of the territory where his ancestors had dwelt.

---

[108] *The Origin of Tithing,* Internet; accessed 28 December 2017; available from
http://www.letusreason.org/doct54.htm

TITHE: A 10% Tax Levy

Remember that a 'tithe' simply means 'one-tenth.' Tithe was generally a ten percent annual tax levied by the owner of a property to the user of such property. The Pharaoh of Egypt demanded the Egyptians a 20% tax because he owned the farmland in which the people grew their crops. Yahweh demanded a tithe from the children of Israel because he owned the land they lived in. In contrast, pastors of some local churches demand members of their congregation 10% of the latter's income even though these pastors do not own the sources from which the people get their income. Since ministers of the gospel are not commanded to charge the followers of Christ in their congregation 10% of the latter's income, the amount charged cannot be termed "biblical tithe." It is simply a 10% tax imposed on the brethren for being a member of the local church in question. In a moment, we will show the gross disparity between the tax levied by Pharaoh and that imposed by leaders of local churches.

During the period of famine in Egypt, Joseph had bought all the lands in Egypt for his master, Pharaoh. He later displaced the people into the cities and gave them seeds to plant in the land (now Pharaoh's). The people were to render unto Pharaoh one-fifth (20%) of the produce of the land and keep the remainder (four-fifth, i.e. 80%) for themselves.

Genesis 47:20-25

20 So Joseph bought all the land in Egypt for Pharaoh. The Egyptians, one and all, sold their fields, because the famine was too severe for them. The land became Pharaoh's,

21 and Joseph reduced the people to servitude, from one end of Egypt to the other.

22 However, he did not buy the land of the priests, because they received a regular allotment from Pharaoh and had food enough from the allotment Pharaoh gave them. That is why they did not sell their land.

23 Joseph said to the people, "Now that I have bought you and your land today for Pharaoh, here is seed for you so you can plant the ground.

24 But when the crop comes in, give a fifth of it to Pharaoh. The other four-fifths you may keep as seed for the fields and as food for yourselves and your households and your children."

25 "You have saved our lives," they said. "May we find favor in the eyes of our lord; we will be in bondage to Pharaoh."

PHARAOH's TAX vs. CHURCH TITHE

The table below shows the gross disparity between Pharaoh's tax (as shown in Genesis 47 above) and the tithe imposed by most churches.

A COMPARISON BETWEEN THE TAX OF PHARAOH & THE TITHE OF THE CHURCH			
SN	DETAIL	PHARAOH's TAX	CHURCH TITHE
1	PERCENTAGE CHARGED	20% of the farmer's harvest (vv. 24).	10% of the church member's income.
2	CAPITAL PROVISION	Land provided to farmers (vv. 23).	No capital provided
3	CAPITAL SUPPORT	Pharaoh provided seeds to plant (vv. 23).	No capital support
4	JUSTIFICATION OF TAX	The king owned the land (vv. 20)	Unjustified by legal & biblical grounds
5	EXEMPTION	Exempts the priests (vv. 22).	Exempts no one.
6	WELFARE	Pharaoh took care of the priests even though the priests did not pay in any tax revenues to Pharaoh (vv. 22).	In some churches, those who do not pay tithes cannot receive church support. In other churches, they are fired.
7	SATISFACTION	100% satisfied. The Egyptians expressed their satisfaction (vv. 25).	Dissatisfied. The high rate of abstinence as revealed by polls indicates disapproval.

Chapter

7

A DISSECTION OF MALACHI 3

Malachi 3:8-10 is a key passage that church leaders use to manipulate the members in their congregation into paying tithes. It is a gross disservice to the biblical gospel to build a doctrine from a prophet's message whose principal parts have been intentionally cut off by the preacher. The audience to whom the message recorded in Malachi 3:8-10 is found nowhere but in Malachi 2. So, to fully understand Malachi 3:8-10, we have to start from the base. In the following lines, we are going to analyze chapter two. Only then can we understand Malachi 3:8-10.

MALACHI 2

Malachi 2:1

¹ "And now, you priests, this warning is for you."

Point 1 (Malachi 2:1):

> ✓ **God addressing the Jewish Priests, not Christians.**

As we can see in verse one above, the Lord God was addressing the Jewish priests of the old covenant, not the Christians of the new covenant. And this address leads up to Malachi 3:8-10, and beyond.

Point 2 (Malachi 2:2-3):

> ✓ **The priests warned of a curse.**

Malachi 2:2-3

² If you do not listen, and if you do not resolve to honor my name," says the LORD Almighty, "I will send a curse on you, and I will curse your blessings. Yes, I have already cursed them, because you have not resolved to honor me.

³ "Because of you I will rebuke your descendants; I will smear on your faces the dung from your festival sacrifices, and you will be carried off with it.

In verse two, the Lord promises to send the Jewish priests a curse if they do not change their ways. The blessings of the priests, which, as we have seen before, are the Lord's portion of the sacrifices and offerings that were to be brought to the altar, will be cursed if these priests do not make a U-turn from their disobedient ways and serve the Lord.

Point 3 (Malachi 2:4-7):

> ✓ **The purpose of the warning was to strengthen the Levitical Covenant**

Malachi 2:4-7

⁴ And you will know that I have sent you this warning so that my covenant with Levi may continue," says the LORD Almighty.

⁵ "My covenant was with him, a covenant of life and peace, and I gave them to him; this called for reverence and he revered me and stood in awe of my name.

⁶ True instruction was in his mouth and nothing false was found on his lips. He walked with me in peace and uprightness, and turned many from sin.

⁷ "For the lips of a priest ought to preserve knowledge, because he is the messenger of the LORD Almighty and people seek instruction from his mouth.

Since the priests operated under the Levitical Covenant, they had to obey the laws of the covenant for the covenant to remain valid or binding. Breaking the laws was synonymous to breaking the covenant. So, the Lord warns them to return by obeying the laws, ordinances, and commandments of the covenant.

Point 4 (Malachi 2:8-13):

✓   The priests and the people became corrupt.

Malachi 2:8-13

⁸ But you have turned from the way and by your teaching have caused many to stumble; you have violated the covenant with Levi," says the LORD Almighty.

⁹ "So I have caused you to be despised and humiliated before all the people, because you have not followed my ways but have shown partiality in matters of the law."

¹⁰ Do we not all have one Father? Did not one God create us? Why do we profane the covenant of our ancestors by being unfaithful to one another?

¹¹ Judah has been unfaithful. A detestable thing has been committed in Israel and in Jerusalem: Judah has desecrated the sanctuary the LORD loves by marrying women who worship a foreign god.

¹² As for the man who does this, whoever he may be, may the LORD remove him from the tents of Jacob—even though he brings an offering to the LORD Almighty.

¹³ Another thing you do: You flood the LORD's altar with tears. You weep and wail because he no longer looks with favor on your offerings or accepts them with pleasure from your hands.

The priests had started drifting away from the true message of the Word of God. They did not rebuke the sins of the people as they should have done (Malachi 2:8). Both Judah (the Southern kingdom) and Israel (the Northern kingdom) did commit an abomination by marrying those who served a strange god (Malachi 2:11). The priests failed to rebuke the people but rather covered the altar of the Lord with their tears (Malachi 2:13) So, because the priests turned a blind eye to the people's sins, the Lord made them to be humiliated by the children of Israel (Malachi 2:9).

In the next page, we are going to dissect Malachi 3, starting from the first verse.

MALACHI 3

Point 1 (Malachi 3:1-3):

> ✓ **The messenger of the new covenant will put order in the house of God.**

Malachi 3:1-3

¹ I will send my messenger, who will prepare the way before me. Then suddenly the Lord you are seeking will come to his temple; the messenger of the covenant, whom you desire, will come," says the LORD Almighty.

² But who can endure the day of his coming? Who can stand when he appears? For he will be like a refiner's fire or a launderer's soap.

³ He will sit as a refiner and purifier of silver; he will purify the Levites and refine them like gold and silver. Then the LORD will have men who will bring offerings in righteousness,

Because of the unfaithfulness of the children of Israel, and the priests' attitude of compromise of the Word of God, as we have seen in the previous chapter, the Lord is announcing to His people, and to the priests in particular, that He is going to send them a messenger who "shall prepare the way" before the coming of the Lord. This servant of the Lord, who would be sent before the coming of the Messiah, is described here as the messenger of the covenant, presumably the new covenant because the Jews had been operating under the old covenant. The description of this messenger indicates he is John the Baptist. The work of this messenger is to purify the sons of Levi by purging them of their former ways so they may serve God diligently and offer acceptable sacrifices. And many of these Jewish priests became converted when they heard the message of the gospel from God's messengers, the Twelve Apostles, as chronicled in Acts 6:7, stated here-below (NIV):

Acts 6:7

⁷ So the word of God spread. The number of disciples in Jerusalem increased rapidly, and a large number of priests became obedient to the faith.

Because our focus in this book is on tithing, we began our analysis from Malachi 2 since it is the foundation of Malachi 3:8-10, the famous passage used by pro-tithe preachers. However, we will suggest that you also read chapter one. Reading chapters one and two of Malachi will give you a deeper understanding of why a messenger of reform was promised to the Jews. The children of Israel showed contempt to God by bringing into God's altar defiled sacrifices such

as blind, crippled, and diseased animals (Malachi 1:7-8). They complained it was too hard for them to serve the Lord (Malachi 1:13).

Point 2 (Malachi 3:4):

> ✓ **The unrighteousness of the priest defiles the sacrifices on the altar.**

Malachi 3:4

⁴ and the offerings of Judah and Jerusalem will be acceptable to the LORD, as in days gone by, as in former years.

It is only when the priests must have been purged and reformed by the messenger of the (new) covenant that sacrifices offered by them, on behalf of Israel, will be acceptable by God. The implication here is that even though the children of Israel honored God by bringing their offerings into God's house, these offerings were not pleasant to the Lord due to the fact that the priests, because of their unrighteous lives, were not perceived to be holy by the Lord. According to the Law of Moses, when the priest sinned, he brought guilt on the entire Jewish community (Leviticus 4:3). Since the offerings were not pleasant to the Lord, it is logical to assume that they did not engender any blessings for those on whose behalf they were offered. That is the reason why in Malachi 3:14 they questioned their service to God. Their offerings did not yield any expected harvests because of their unrighteous lives. Thus, their unrighteousness did repel God from showing Himself mighty in their midst.

Point 3 (Malachi 3:5-6):

> ✓ **Iniquity shall be judged**

Malachi 3:5-6

⁵ "So I will come to put you on trial. I will be quick to testify against sorcerers, adulterers and perjurers, against those who defraud laborers of their wages, who oppress the widows and the fatherless, and deprive the foreigners among you of justice, but do not fear me," says the LORD Almighty.

⁶ "I the LORD do not change. So you, the descendants of Jacob, are not destroyed.

The Lord highlights some of the iniquities of the people: witchcraft, adultery, false swearing, cheating workers of their wages, oppressing the widows and orphans, and depriving foreigners of justice. He promised that those who perpetrate such sinful acts were going to be judged.

Point 4 (Malachi 3:7):

> ✓ **Tithing was an ordinance.**

Malachi 3:7-9

[7] Ever since the time of your ancestors you have turned away from my decrees and have not kept them. Return to me, and I will return to you," says the LORD Almighty. "But you ask, 'How are we to return?'

[8] "Will a mere mortal rob God? Yet you rob me. "But you ask, 'How are we robbing you?' "In tithes and offerings.

[9] You are under a curse—your whole nation—because you are robbing me.

The Lord reminds the children of Israel that since the days of their ancestors, they had always drifted away from following His ordinances. He beckoned on Israel to return unto Him so that He the Lord would also return unto them. Returning, on the part of Israel, here means "Renew your observance of the ordinances I had given you through my servant, Moses." The Lord went further to mention *tithes* as one of those ordinances He wanted Israel to return to. Thus, tithing was an ordinance.

Remember that we have stated in the introduction of this book that tithing is no more applicable to Christians because Christians are not under the Law but under Grace. As an ordinance, tithing is under the Law of Moses. The Jews, not Christians, were mandated to follow the commandments and ordinances of the Law. That is the reason why Jesus, in Matthew 23:23, did not rebuke the Jews for their practice of tithing (we will visit that passage shortly). In fact, it is catastrophic for Christians who are under the new covenant, regulated by GRACE, to follow the recommendations of the Law of Moses.

Point 5 (Malachi 3:8):

> ✓ **Not tithing equated to robbing God.**

The Lord qualifies the Jew's act of not bringing tithes and offerings into His house as an act of robbery. Why does God describe this phenomenon as robbery? Remember that the land that was given to the children of Israel was God's. They did not acquire the land with any material payment. They only fought those who had inhabited the land, while God gave them victory. So, the Lord God had told them from the onset that a tenth of the produce of the land belonged to Him. It is holy unto the Lord. It should not be utilized for any other purposes. This tenth portion, otherwise called *tithe*, was actually given to the Levites as their inheritance, as we had explained before.

A Jew who does not bring a tenth of their harvested crops to the temple of God will be robbing God of His holy portion. However, the same cannot be said today of a Christian because Christians, who are non-Jews, do not fall under the same land scheme as did the Jews.

Why "Offering" Was Manipulatively Eliminated from Being Termed "Robbing God"

Also, note that in verse 8, it was not only the aspect of not tithing that was equated to robbing God. It is clearly stated in that verse that the Jews had robbed God "in tithes and offerings." Pastors that accuse their members of being robbers of God do so in reference to tithes only. They do this manipulatively. Do you know why? If they do include 'offerings' as mentioned in the passage, it will land them into a big trouble. *Offerings* as mentioned in that verse included *burnt offering* (Leviticus 1), *grain offering* (Leviticus 2), *peace offering* (Leviticus 3), *sin offering* (Leviticus 4), and *guilt offering* (Leviticus 5). When the Jews brought to the Temple the *sin offering*, for example, the priest must eat a certain portion of it in a sacred place within the Tabernacle. The Jews were commanded by God to bring the above-mentioned offerings to the Temple depending on the circumstance. The item that was offered at the altar belonged to God. Therefore, when the children of Israel failed to bring these offerings to the house of God, like tithes, they were robbing God of what belonged to Him.

Let us now see why pro-tithe pastors will not cite the 'offerings' mentioned in Malachi 3:8. Let us consider one scenario with respect to The Sin Offering. When a leader in Israel did sin by breaking the Law of Moses, he presented to the altar a male goat as an offering for his sin. He then placed his hand on the goat's head while slaughtering it, after which the priest will dip his finger on the blood and rub it on the horns of the altar reserved for burnt offerings. By this ritual, the Jewish leader was cleansed of his sin, as shown below:

Leviticus 4:22-26

[22] "When a leader sins unintentionally and does what is forbidden in any of the commands of the LORD his God, when he realizes his guilt

23 and the sin he has committed becomes known, he must bring as his offering a male goat without defect.

24 He is to lay his hand on the goat's head and slaughter it at the place where the burnt offering is slaughtered before the LORD. It is a sin offering.

25 Then the priest shall take some of the blood of the sin offering with his finger and put it on the horns of the altar of burnt offering and pour out the rest of the blood at the base of the altar.

26 He shall burn all the fat on the altar as he burned the fat of the fellowship offering. In this way the priest will make atonement for the leader's sin, and he will be forgiven."

Now, it will be an abomination for any pastor to demand their congregation to bring along a goat or any other animal as their sin offering. It will be more of an abomination for the said pastor to perform the cleansing ritual by slaughtering the animal and sprinkling its blood on a place in the church auditorium. This is because as Christians, we have been cleansed from our sins by the blood of God's own Son, Jesus Christ. Do you now understand why a pastor who collects tithes will not mention the non-payment of "offerings" in the context of Malachi 3:8 as an act of robbing God? Old covenant practices were simply a shadow of the new covenant. The new has come, the old must disappear.

Point 6 (Malachi 3:10):

✓   **Tithes were stored in the storehouse of the Temple.**

Malachi 3:10

10 "Bring the whole tithe into the storehouse, that there may be food in my house. Test me in this," says the LORD Almighty, "and see if I will not throw open the floodgates of heaven and pour out so much blessing that there will not be room enough to store it."

Again, verse 10 highlights the fact that tithes were kept in a special chamber of the Temple, otherwise called *storehouse*. And these tithes were food items, not physical cash. The expression, "that there may be meat in mine house" indicates that the tithes were food for the workers of the Temple (the priests and Levites).

As the shutting up of heaven indicates scarcity, the "opening of the windows of heaven" is a proverbial language used to express God's showering down of abundant blessings of the fruits of the field. The Jews were promised abundant rains if they obeyed the commands of the Lord, as recorded in Deuteronomy 11:13-15 here below:

Deuteronomy 11:13-15

[13] "So if you faithfully obey the commands I am giving you today—to love the LORD your God and to serve him with all your heart and with all your soul—

[14] then I will send rain on your land in its season, both autumn and spring rains, so that you may gather in your grain, new wine and olive oil.

[15] I will provide grass in the fields for your cattle, and you will eat and be satisfied."

It should be noted that a portion of the tithe received by the priest was brought to the storehouse. The male priests were commanded to eat this portion inside the holy places of the storehouse (see Numbers 18:10). The tithe of the Levites (90% of the tithes received from the non-Levitical tribes) was NEVER brought to the storehouse. So, they were allowed to eat it in the place of their choice (see Numbers 18:31). This agrees with Nehemiah 10:37 commanding Israel to bring tithes to the Levitical cities and not to the temple storehouse at Jerusalem. Thus Malachi 3:10, Kelly argues, refers only to the "tenth of tithe," the portion brought from the Levitical cities into the storehouse. [109]

Point 7 (Malachi 3:11-12):

✓   **A divine conditional promise made to the Jews.**

Malachi 3:11-12

[11] "I will prevent pests from devouring your crops, and the vines in your fields will not drop their fruit before it is ripe," says the LORD Almighty.

[12] "Then all the nations will call you blessed, for yours will be a delightful land," says the LORD Almighty.

To motivate the Jews to bring their tithes and offerings into the house of God, as commanded, so that the Levites and priests can have enough food to enable them do the work of the Lord, the God of the Jews is making a new promise of oversight over their crops. However, this promise is conditioned on the premise that the Jews bring their tithes into the storehouse. That is, when the Jews bring into the house of God a tenth of the harvested crops of their given portion of land, the Lord God was going to protect the remaining nine-tenth from any unforeseeable force of destruction. As a result, the blessings of the Jews will be more outstanding with respect to that of their pagan neighbors.

---

[109] Kelly, *Should the Church Teach Tithing?* 38.

Point 8 (Malachi 3:13-15):

> ✓ **The Jews questioned the worth of their service.**

Malachi 3:13-15

[13] "You have spoken arrogantly against me," says the LORD. "Yet you ask, 'What have we said against you?'

[14] "You have said, 'It is futile to serve God. What do we gain by carrying out his requirements and going about like mourners before the LORD Almighty?

[15] But now we call the arrogant blessed. Certainly evildoers prosper, and even when they put God to the test, they get away with it.'"

The Jews had become wearied of serving the Lord. So, they questioned the value of their service and obedience. And they concluded that it was vain to serve the Lord God. This led to a kind of apostasy whereby evil was upheld as good.

Therefore, as we have seen so far, Malachi 3 was not addressed to Christians. It was addressed mainly to the Jewish priests/Levites, <u>not</u> to followers of Christ. No Christian is cursed by God for not paying tithes. This is because no Christian is under the Law that legitimized the payment of tithes in the order of the old covenant.

A PLAUSIBLE ORIGIN OF THE CURSE OF NON-TITHING

There is a possibility that the famous curse associated with non-tithing duly recorded in Malachi 3:9 might have originated from the Israelites themselves, and not from their God, Yahweh. By declaring, "You are under a curse, for your whole nation has been cheating me," it was likely that Yahweh was simply pronouncing the judgment on the oath the Israelites had taken to tithe, which they ended up desecrating.

The Children of Israel Took an Oath to Tithe

Nehemiah 10:28-39 below gives us the narrative of the children of Israel who unanimously took an oath to follow all the commands of the LORD (including the command to tithe in verse 37) invoking a curse on themselves should they break their oath.

Nehemiah 10:28-39

[28] "The rest of the people—priests, Levites, gatekeepers, musicians, temple servants and all who separated themselves from the neighboring peoples for the sake of the Law of God, together with their wives and all their sons and daughters who are able to understand—

29 all these now join their fellow Israelites the nobles, and bind themselves with a curse and an oath to follow the Law of God given through Moses the servant of God and to obey carefully all the commands, regulations and decrees of the LORD our Lord.

30 "We promise not to give our daughters in marriage to the peoples around us or take their daughters for our sons.

31 "When the neighboring peoples bring merchandise or grain to sell on the Sabbath, we will not buy from them on the Sabbath or on any holy day. Every seventh year we will forgo working the land and will cancel all debts.

32 "We assume the responsibility for carrying out the commands to give a third of a shekel each year for the service of the house of our God:

33 for the bread set out on the table; for the regular grain offerings and burnt offerings; for the offerings on the Sabbaths, at the New Moon feasts and at the appointed festivals; for the holy offerings; for sin offerings to make atonement for Israel; and for all the duties of the house of our God.

34 "We—the priests, the Levites and the people—have cast lots to determine when each of our families is to bring to the house of our God at set times each year a contribution of wood to burn on the altar of the LORD our God, as it is written in the Law.

35 "We also assume responsibility for bringing to the house of the LORD each year the firstfruits of our crops and of every fruit tree.

36 "As it is also written in the Law, we will bring the firstborn of our sons and of our cattle, of our herds and of our flocks to the house of our God, to the priests ministering there.

37 "Moreover, we will bring to the storerooms of the house of our God, to the priests, the first of our ground meal, of our grain offerings, of the fruit of all our trees and of our new wine and olive oil. And we will bring a tithe of our crops to the Levites, for it is the Levites who collect the tithes in all the towns where we work.

38 A priest descended from Aaron is to accompany the Levites when they receive the tithes, and the Levites are to bring a tenth of the tithes up to the house of our God, to the storerooms of the treasury.

39 The people of Israel, including the Levites, are to bring their contributions of grain, new wine and olive oil to the storerooms, where the articles for the sanctuary and for the ministering priests, the gatekeepers and the musicians are also kept.
"We will not neglect the house of our God."

Note that during this time, the Jews had been living under siege. They were being ruled by a foreign king because they had disobeyed the Lord their God (Nehemiah 9:32-38). So, they made a vow to return to the Lord their God, placing a curse on themselves in case they break their vow. Tithing was among the laws they had vowed to obey. Therefore, when Malachi 3:9 said the children of Israel were under a curse for failing to bring the tithes and offerings into the storehouse, it seems God was simply reminding the Jews of the consequence of the promise they themselves had made in Nehemiah 10:28-39.

WHY TITHING IS NOT FOR THE CHURCH

Two Testaments, Two Covenants: Old and New

The Christian Bible is made up of two main sections, which we call Testaments: Old Testament + New Testament. The Old Testament is governed by the underlying principles of the old covenant meanwhile the New Testament is governed by the new covenant principles. The Old Testament was a shadow of the New Testament meanwhile the New Testament is a revelation of the Old Testament. To understand the Bible correctly, it is imperative that the reader of Scripture understands the conditions, principles, and context under which each Testament was written.

The Old Testament, in which era the law of tithing was given, must be understood in light of the customs and practices that governed the people living in the Ancient Near East. On this, Kitchen writes,

> "Now geographically, historically, and culturally, the Ancient Near East *is* the world of the Old Testament, while humanly speaking the Old Testament is a part of Ancient Near Eastern literature, history and culture. Therefore, what can be known about the history, literatures, linguistics, religion, etc., of the Ancient Orient will have a *direct bearing* upon these same aspects of the Old Testament." [110]

Bearing the above in mind, the doctrine of financial giving in the Church must be practiced on the basis of sound biblical exegesis. No

---

[110] Wretlind, *Shekels, Dollars, and Sense*, 7.

follower of Christ should listen to a preacher who tells them to stone to death their child for blaspheming the name of God (Leviticus 24:16), for not honoring the Sabbath (Exodus 31:15), for worshipping false gods (Deuteronomy 13:6-10), for committing homosexuality (Leviticus 20:13), for committing adultery (Leviticus 20:10), for practicing witchcraft (Leviticus 20:27), or for being disobedient to parents (Deuteronomy 21:18-21) simply because these things are written in the Old Testament section of the Bible. As a matter of biblical principle, since the New Testament is a fulfillment of the Old Testament, the Old Testament must be interpreted in the eyes of the New Testament (I encourage you to read Matthew 5:38-48. This will give you a glimpse of how different the old covenant system is from the new).

THE NEW COVENANT HAS FULFILLED THE OLD

Romans 10:4 (NLT)

[4] For Christ has already accomplished the purpose for which the law was given. As a result, all who believe in him are made right with God.

It should be underlined that the new covenant, embodied by the New Testament section of the Bible, was given to the followers of Christ to be a fulfillment of the old covenant, a covenant the Hebrews could not fulfill by the works of the Law. This new covenant we are talking about states unequivocally (see Ephesians 2:8-9) that our salvation comes from the grace of God through our faith in God's son, Jesus Christ, alone, and not from the works of the Law such as tithing, first-fruits, circumcision, etc.

Since the Mosaic Covenant has been fulfilled by Christ, the follower of Christ is not bound by the constituent laws of that covenant such as tithing. On this issue Wretlind adds,

> "One also needs to add that the 'tithing-offering systems of Judaism' is integrally related to the Mosaic Covenant, a Covenant done away in Christ (Hebrews 8)." [111]

Who will continue to stick onto their old business arrangement when a new, more profitable, and flexible one has been provided for zero cost? It takes only a complete ignorance of the comparative advantage of the new business arrangement on the part of an entrepreneur for such a scenario to occur.

---

[111] Wretlind, *Shekels, Dollars, and Sense*, 22.

"When lower interest rates are available, many people refinance their homes. But again, WHO WOULD CONTINUE TO LIVE BY THEIR 'OLD' MORTGAGE COVENANT AFTER IT HAS BEEN 'PAID' AND REPLACED BY A 'NEW' TOTALLY PAID DEED? Sadly, this scenario describes the spiritual condition and understanding of the church today. They are trying to live by both covenants. Every single day, obsolete OT principles are taught to the church as 'gospel,' but few give it a second thought because 'it came from the Bible' and it was mixed with NT verses.

One of the covenants in the Bible brings a blessing or a curse, depending on how you perform, while the other brings blessings as free gifts. One requires 10 percent of your increase, while the other is freely given. One was implemented under the Law of Moses long before Jesus was born, while the other was set in place after Jesus fulfilled the Law and nailed it to His cross.

One is the Old Covenant providing benefits for man depending upon man's performance, while the other is the New Covenant, which provides benefits for man based on Jesus' performance. One is GRACE; the other is WORKS, which would include tithing, circumcision, keeping the Sabbath, animal sacrifices, and many other such things." [112]

So why is understanding the differences between the two covenants important? It is because we cannot practice the demands of both at the same time. In other words, we cannot be married to both covenants. As shown above, in one covenant (the old), righteousness was achieved through THE LAW. In the other (new) covenant, righteousness is achieved through GRACE. So, practicing THE LAW of the old covenant while at the same time embracing the GRACE of the new covenant will end up frustrating the GRACE of God that's on the believer's life (Galatians 2:21) leading to DISGRACE. As a result, the righteousness of Christ needed by the believer to achieve their salvation will be far-fetched. That's why we have to make a choice. For followers of Christ, embracing the new covenant system is the only option if they are to reap the eternal blessings of the finished work of Christ on the cross.

Caught between Two Covenants

Absalom's fatal death reminds us of the position most Christians find themselves today. On a horse in pursuit of his father, David, for elimination, Absalom's thick and long hair was caught by a tree leaving him dead, and hanging between the heaven and the earth. The Bible calls Absalom's place of death "the place of cursing." The place was named that way because it was neither connected to the heaven nor the earth. [113] Our savior, Jesus Christ, also died in a place between the heaven and the earth. However, Christ died for our sins, not his own. Like Absalom, Wells writes, many Christians are caught

---

[112] Wells, *The Great Tithing Debate*, 2.
[113] Ibid., 12.

between two covenants (old/new) with virtually no defense. The Christians who are caught between the old and the new covenants really don't know what to do because they do not know which covenant governs their situation.

You Can't Have It Both Ways!

Recall that Eritrea and Ethiopia were once one country. However, after the thirty-year Eritrean War of Independence (1 September 1961 - 29 May 1991), Eritrea became a new country. No matter the historical ties that existed between these two countries, they are two separate countries today with well-defined boundaries and distinct territorial laws. Once you're in Ethiopia, you're bound by the laws of Ethiopia. The same is true for Eritrea. But, today, you can't live in the new country (Eritrea) and apply the laws of the mother country (Ethiopia) and expect not to be prosecuted by the Eritrean judiciary. As a matter of fact, behaving in such a manner is tantamount to insanity. The same is true for any Christian who chooses to exercise, in the profession of their faith, the laws of the old covenant even though they find themselves in the new covenant dispensation.

Also recall that in the days of Paul, to be admitted into the membership of a local church, the followers of Christ were compelled to practice circumcision. Today, circumcision is no longer a barrier to church membership. However, *tithing* is. In some churches, followers of Christ are being compelled to tithe in order to be accepted as full members of X or Y church. This is a sad phenomenon that engulfs the Body of Christ today.

As far as the Church is concerned, the only covenant the Lord God Almighty does honor is the new covenant, a covenant that was ratified by the blood of His Son, Jesus Christ, who doubles as the Head of the Church.

Do you know that most Christians who pay tithes are not even aware of the fact that tithing was an old covenant law? Since tithing provides a source of income to the church, they reason, God surely endorses the payment of tithes and must be delighted with the tithe payers for supporting His church.

Note that Paul referred to the old covenant as "the covenant of death." Paul continually warned the Church of circumcision because by practicing it, like tithing, it brings the believer under the curse of the Law.

Many things may go wrong when church leaders start looking up to their congregation as their source of funding. When the minister's focus is shifted from the true Head of the Church to its Body, the ministry becomes powerless. If you look around, there are many churches that look so successful from the outside, but they are a big failure in terms of the impact they make in the community that's around them. They are so powerful in the material realm but very powerless in the spiritual. Why? Misplaced priorities! Seek ye **first** 'the kingdom of God and his righteousness.'

TITHING: AN ABOLISHED LAW

As per Dispensational theology, the old covenant, the Mosaic Law, the commandments, ordinances, and judgments form one and indivisible revelation, which belong to old covenant Israel. Only those laws that have been restated in the wording of the new covenant have been passed on to the Church. Also, Kelly continues, "Tithing was not mentioned as an 'exception' to the rule decreed by the Jerusalem church leaders in the book of Acts." [114]

> "The tithing ordinance was one of the many ordinances which made sharp distinctions between Hebrew and Gentile, and, of necessity, must be abolished if the church were to be united into one spiritual organism. Tithes were food only to be received from Hebrew landowners and herdsmen inside the sacred land of Israel. Ordinances defined the daily lives of every Hebrew person and ordinances defined everything the priest was and did." [115]

Tithing created the priesthood. So, if you tithe you are enacting what had been destroyed. At the very heart of the Mosaic Law was tithing (duly worded by Numbers 18).

Gentiles Did Not Qualify to Pay Tithes

Gentiles did not qualify under the ordinances as tithe payers. In the old covenant, Gentiles could never be considered as God's people. They could not inherit God's land and thus had no holy land from which to pay tithes.

Gentiles who became circumcised as proselytes were never considered full Jews; they were considered "at the gate." The tithe of a proselyte could not enter the temple. A Jewish priest could not accept a tithe from a non-Jew or from a land considered pagan or

---

[114] Kelly, *Should the Church Teach Tithing?* 174.
[115] Ibid., 172.

defiled.

Thus, tithing was one of those ordinances which constituted a wall between Jews and Gentiles. When Christ came, he broke down this wall by abolishing tithing through his death and resurrection.

It is interesting to note that the Jewish priests got only a tiny fraction of the tithes - just 1%:

> Surprising and shocking to many, the most important preachers, or ministers in the Old Covenant did NOT receive the tithes. They only received one tenth of the tithe from their Levite servants. Also, the Temple shekel and freewill offerings covered the expenses of building and maintaining the Temple and purchasing the animals for the nation's sacrifices. [116]

Talking about the office of a pastor, Kelly writes:

> "The 'pastor-teacher' of the New Covenant church fills an entirely new office not found in the Old Covenant rules for priests (Heb. 7:14-15). This office does NOT exist because of Mosaic Law provisions, but functions under principles of grace and faith (Heb. 7:16). Since the connection is not linear (straight-line), there is no Scriptural justification for shifting law-tithing from Old Covenant priests to the pastor-teachers. In fact, there is Scriptural justification for *not* transferring the tithe obligations from Old Covenant priests to New Covenant pastor-teachers (Heb. 7:14-19)....The New Covenant pastor-teacher has more in common with the Old Covenant prophet, and, later, the rabbi, than its priest. Many Old Covenant prophets were not Levites. They ministered by faith, depending on God's provisions and their own hands at a trade. Therefore, it is erroneous to act as if the New Covenant pastor took up where the Old Covenant Levitical priest left off and is, therefore, due the priest's tithe." [117]

TITHING: NOT A CHRISTIAN DOCTRINE!

The reason why most believers still fall prey to the practice of the old covenant law of tithing is largely due to their ignorance of what tithing was. In 1 Corinthians 2:13, Paul, the apostle to the Gentiles, encourages us to elucidate, uncover or interpret spiritual things by using the same words we have been taught by the Spirit. And by 'the words taught us by the Spirit' we are referring here to the Word of God. In this section, we will show you some biblical evidence why tithing is not, and cannot be, a doctrine for the New Testament Church.

---

[116] Kelly, *Should the Church Teach Tithing?* 36.
[117] Ibid., 180.

WHY TITHING IN THE CHURCH IS WRONG!

[NEW TESTAMENT (NT) EVIDENCE]

1. MATTHEW

Point 1 (Matthew 6:1):

✓   **Tithing contradicts the NT Principle of 'Giving in Secret.'**

Matthew 6:1 (NLT)

[1] "Watch out! Don't do your good deeds publicly, to be admired by others, for you will lose the reward from your Father in heaven."

One of the reasons why tithing is disqualified as a credible doctrine of giving in the church is because it is not a giving in secret. Alms, as expressed in Matthew 6:1, generally refer to money or food given to people who do not have them. And tithing, as we have said before, is the Jewish practice whereby the non-Levitical tribes of Israel had to give a tenth of their cultivated crops and/or reared animals to the Levites who had been given no portion of the Promised Land where they could grow their own crops. When a Jew gave their tithe, it was received by one of the appointed treasurers and kept in a chamber, as recorded in Nehemiah 12:44. Since tithing is giving alms to the Levites and since it is not a giving in secret, it does not comply with the standard of New Testament giving. Therefore, tithing cannot be a doctrine for giving in the Church.

The introductory clause "Take heed" implies "Be careful!" Whenever the Lord Jesus Christ uses this clause in Scripture, he is beseeching us to pay a special attention to what is said following the clause: "do not your alms before men, to be seen of them."

Point 2 (Matthew 6:1):

✓   **Tithing brings no rewards under the new covenant.**

Given that tithing does violate the New Testament principle of "giving in secret," it, therefore, does not convey any rewards to the giver. As a matter of fact, Christ makes this point very clearly in Matthew 6:1 by saying that if you give your alms before men you will have no rewards from your heavenly Father.

Some may argue, "But I do not announce to anyone when I pay my tithe. I simply quietly drop it in the offering/tithe basket of the church. So, my tithe should produce a heavenly reward for me." If you have read this book from the beginning, we presume that you should have known by now what tithing was all about, why it was created, and who should pay tithes according to the Law of Moses. That notwithstanding, ignorance of a law is never an excuse. Paying tithes in the church, whether publicly or in secret, it should be underlined, brings no rewards because tithing was an ordinance given to the Jews, not to Christians. It is a defunct doctrine as far as the Church of Christ is concerned.

Point 3 (Matthew 6:2):

> ✓ **Tithing installs pride in the giver's heart.**

Matthew 6:2 (NLT)

[2] "When you give to someone in need, don't do as the hypocrites do – blowing trumpets in the synagogues and streets to call attention to their acts of charity! I tell you the truth, they have received all the reward they will ever get."

One of the reasons why tithing was never endorsed by Christ and his apostles is because it bestows pride in the giver's heart. Through their act of tithing, which they see as a form of benevolence toward God, the giver of tithes sees themselves as God's partner, collaborator or helper. When they pay tithes into their local church, the tithe payer, in a subtle way, beats their hand on their chest, saying to themselves "Without me this church might not survive." Their strength is in the amount of money they give as tithes, not in the grace of God. Such Christians would want to be in control of the way the church should be run, even to the extent of making recommendations of what message should be preached or not.

I have heard some pastors going to the extent of telling members of their congregation that when they pay their tithes, it is the tithe payers' right to demand God to step into their affairs during times of trouble, and calm down the storms as God had promised in Malachi 3. This is a display of extreme legalism, or, we should say, God-hunt! They tell the gullible tithe payers to gather every proof of their tithe payment records, lift them up to the heavens, and invoke God to come down and do something about their prevailing situation. In fact, I have been a witness to such clerical calls in my then local church.

With regards to such attitudes by pastors, Rolston writes, "There is a grave danger that in the preaching of the tithe we shall fall into a type of legalism which is not essentially different from the Jewish legalism which Paul rebelled against." [118]

Point 4 (Matthew 6:3-4):

> ✓ **Tithing breaches top secrecy in giving.**

Matthew 6:3-4 (NLT)

[3] "But when you give to someone in need, don't let your left hand know what your right hand is doing.

[4] Give your gifts in private, and your Father, who sees everything, will reward you."

"Don't let your left hand know what your right hand is doing" is a proverbial expression, which indicates top secrecy in the giving of alms. To be fair, no one can give without actually knowing the content and size of their giving. This is a common fact. However, that is not what the Lord is saying here. In this passage, the Lord Jesus is simply warning us against any outward shows in our giving habit. That is, we should give in such a way that if it were possible, we might not know what we give, talk less of letting others know of it. The expression is not just proverbial, but it is hyperbolical as well. The message our Lord Jesus is conveying here is that any giving under the new covenant must be "a top secret." Tithing breaches this characteristic as somebody must be aware of the amount of money that a church member usually submits to their local church as tithe (10% of giver's income). The exact amount of tithes is known either by the pastor, the elder, or the church clerk who records the figures in a journal entry. As an accountant of a church, it was my duty to write down the names of church members who paid their tithes into the church. I somehow felt bad about this, but because I didn't know any better, I had no choice. It is for this reason that tithing is quashed as a doctrine for giving in the New Testament Church.

The expression "and your Father, who sees everything, will reward you" indicates two things:

(1) God endorses only those alms that are given in secret.

(2) He only rewards what He endorses.

---

[118] Wretlind, *Shekels, Dollars, and Sense*, 4.

Analyzing Matthew 23:23-26

Some have claimed that the practice of tithing in the Church is legitimate because Jesus mentioned tithing in Matthew 23:23. But what did Jesus say about tithing to warrant its endorsement in the Church? We will now visit that passage and see for ourselves what is said therein. Only by so-doing can we make any informed conclusion regarding this matter.

Matthew 23:23 (KJV)

23 "Woe unto you, scribes and Pharisees, hypocrites! for ye pay tithe of mint and anise and cummin, and have omitted the weightier matters of the law, judgment, mercy, and faith: these ought ye to have done, and not to leave the other undone."

Point 1 (Matthew 23:23):

> ✓ **Jesus recognized tithing under the Law of Moses.**

The first point to note here is that by saying to the scribes and Pharisees that they ought not to leave the other (referring to *tithe*) undone, Jesus was simply recognizing the legitimacy of tithing as inscribed in the Law of Moses. That is, Jesus was simply acknowledging the fact that though tithing was a legitimate obligation of those he was speaking to (the Jews), the practice of judgment, mercy, and faith cannot be sidelined or sacrificed on the platter of tithe-obedience, for the three aspects just mentioned above are "weightier" than tithing in matters relating to the law. Things ought to be done properly. Jesus was simply rebuking the followers of the Law of Moses for not practicing the Law in the proper way.

Point 2 (Matthew 23:23):

> ✓ **Tithing is not the priority in matters of the Law.**

Jesus also made a stunning revelation here: Tithing is not the priority in matters relating to the Law of Moses. Jesus brought out three aspects of the Law: judgment, mercy, and faith, placing these above tithing in a scale of preference in matters relating to spiritual observance. That is to say, Jesus was saying that if a Jew was given an opportunity to choose from the following two options: 'Show mercy to your neighbor' or 'take your tithe to the Temple,' they should embrace the first option and not the second.

Remember that the Old Testament is a shadow of the New. Christians should pursue justice, mercy, and faith over the giving of freewill offerings, not to say that these offerings should be ignored. However, freewill offerings could be ignored if the pursuance of justice, mercy, or faith makes it impossible for the believer to give.

As an example, consider the case of a young Christian who was approached by his sick neighbor for a medical assistance worth $50. The Christian in question turned down the sick on the pretext that he didn't have any money to assist. However, the young Christian was seen the following Sunday dropping into the basket of his local church a $50 note he had reserved as his "offering money." This Christian forfeited showing mercy to his sick neighbor for the sake of giving an offering to the church. The reverse should have been done, according to our Lord Jesus Christ. Such a scenario is pervasive among Christians today. And this was the same attitude Christ was denouncing with regards to the scribes and Pharisees.

Talking about tithing, how many Christians today pay huge sums of money into their local churches every month without caring for the people in their own families, who are suffering from one life challenge to another? The sad thing is that most of the tithe payers do this without any iota of spiritual guilt in them. They are hypocrites, and their consciences have been seared with a hot iron, as 1 Timothy 4:2 puts it.

Point 3 (Matthew 23:23):

✓   **Jesus affirms tithe wasn't money but crops.**

Remember that we had said that tithing was *never about money* but about agricultural produce in the land of Israel. In Matthew 23:23, Jesus is reaffirming this aspect of the ordinance of tithing, as recorded in the Law of Moses.

Tithes Paid from Mint, Anise & Cumin

Jesus said, "For ye pay tithe of mint and anise and cummin." He didn't say, "For ye pay tithe of your monthly wages." What are these: mint, anise, and cummin? These are all agricultural plants. The mint is an aromatic plant, several types of which are used as culinary herbs. The mint oil is used in making candies. Peppermint sweet, for example, is made from the mint oil. Anise seeds are used in cooking. They have a good flavor. They are also used in the manufacture of medicines.

Cumin (KJV spelt *cummin*) is a small, slender plant that bears cumin seeds. The seeds are used as food spices. The curry powder, for example, is made up of cumin seeds.

Point 4 (Matthew 23:23):

> ✓ **Jesus was addressing Jews, not Christians.**

The fourth point to note is that Jesus, in Matthew 23:23, was not speaking to his followers, the Christians, but he was speaking to the Jews. The Jews operated under the old covenant and their religion was Judaism. They were guided by the sacred works of Moses, their prophet, not the Gospel of Jesus. In fact, one of the reasons why the Jews plotted to kill Jesus was because they thought Jesus was desecrating their religious system.

The Christians, on the other hand, function under the new covenant. They fellowship together and are collectively called "the Church." Christ is their head, and their dedication is upholding the message of the kingdom of God, which their master entrusted into their hands. For their eternal salvation, the Christians, unlike the Jews, depend on the grace of their master, and not on the Law of Moses. Since it was the Jews whom Christ was addressing here, it is, therefore, unpalatable for the Christians to put into effect an address that was not intended for them in the first place. The Christians must not do what their Master, through the Gospel, did not command them to do.

Point 5 (Matthew 23:23):

> ✓ **Your tithes cannot make up for your unfaithfulness.**

It should be remarked that even though Christ acknowledged the fact that the scribes and Pharisees did pay their tithes, he, nevertheless, went further to scream, "Woe unto you, scribes and Pharisees, hypocrites!" By saying "woe," Jesus was simply alerting the scribes and Pharisees of the calamity that would befall them for their hypocrisy of trying to cover up the upholding of justice, mercy and faith with the payment of tithes. And this calamity would befall tithe payers in local churches as well who fail to uphold the weightier matters of the law mentioned above due to their practice of tithe-giving. The obedience of the minor good cannot make up for the disobedience or outright neglect of the major good. The great sorrow must come. It cannot be stopped by the tithes of the scribes and

Pharisees; neither can it be stopped by the tithes of the Christians. This passage should serve as a big lesson to Christians who have been made to believe that their tithes will always speak for them in difficult moments even when they fail to exercise faith, show justice and mercy toward their fellow neighbors.

Point 6 (Matthew 23:24):

✓   **Any Christian who pays tithe is a blind sheep.**

Point 7 (Matthew 23:24):

✓   **Any pastor who teaches tithing is a blind shepherd.**

Matthew 23:24 (KJV)

[24] Ye blind guides, which strain at a gnat, and swallow a camel.

For their failure to observe the weightier matters of the Law - justice, mercy, and faith - in favor of tithing, Jesus describes the teachers of the Jewish religious law as "blind guides." By implication, the Jews who gave tithes but did not uphold justice, mercy, and faith were the blind sheep of their teachers. Today, the standards of spiritual devotion have fallen greatly in most churches. Many believers are busy looking for what offerings and sacrifices they can give to God to cause God to bless them financially. To achieve financial blessings, many struggle against all odds to meet up with the demands of tithing. They do this without any concrete spiritual devotion to God, and firm expression of love toward their neighbors. Such Christians, according to the words of Christ in Matthew 23:24, are *the blind sheep of the church*. Those that teach them to prioritize tithe-giving over justice, mercy and faith, collect their tithes and give them preferential treatment or high positions of leadership in the church are *the blind guides/shepherds of the church*.

"Strain at a gnat"

The blind shepherds "strain at a gnat, and swallow a camel." To understand this statement, we need to explain a number of things here. First, "to strain **at** a gnat" makes no sense. This appears to be a misprint. It should have been, as contained in some of the earlier versions of the

Bible, "to strain **out** a gnat."[119] We know that "to strain out" is using a filter to remove a solid substance from a liquid or gas.

A gnat is a small two-winged fly having a sharp sting, and looks like a mosquito. Gnats are usually found in pools and marshes. It appears that to fetch water from a pool, the Jews would have to strain themselves so as to avoid catching any gnats in their vessel. *Gnat* is used here by Jesus to denote a very small matter (tithe) as *a camel* is used to denote a big matter (the non-upholding of justice, mercy, and faith).

> "You Jews take great pains to avoid offence in very small matters, superstitiously observing the smallest points of the law, like a man carefully straining out the animalculae from what he drinks, while you are at no pains to avoid great sins - hypocrisy, deceit, oppression, and lust - like a man who should swallow a camel"[120]

Remember that these three virtues (justice, mercy, and faith) cited by Christ are the very important ingredients that sustain the spiritual life of a believer. Take *faith*, for example. No matter the amount of tithe the believer pays to their local church, if their faith is not connected to Christ they cannot be saved. In the Final Day of Judgment, none will be judged according to how much tithes or offerings they had paid during their lifetime on earth, but we will all be judged according to our faithfulness in upholding justice, mercy, and faith.

Point 8 (Matthew 23:25):

✓   **Tithe is a window-dressing of the heart.**

Matthew 23:25 (KJV)

[25] Woe unto you, scribes and Pharisees, hypocrites! for ye make clean the outside of the cup and of the platter, but within they are full of extortion and excess.

For what they have done, Jesus describes the scribes and Pharisees as "hypocrites." A hypocrite is someone whose actions belie their religious beliefs. The scribes and Pharisees here properly fit this categorization since they didn't do what ought to have been done.

Jesus went further to say that the scribes and Pharisees "make clean the outside of the cup and of the platter, but within they are full of extortion and excess." "Making clean the outside of the cup" refers to tithing. Unfortunately, the inside of the cup is not clean at all; it is full of extortion and excesses of the law. Since the inside of the cup (the

---

[119] Matthew 23:24 commentary, under 'Barnes' Notes on the Bible; Internet; accessed 10 October 2020; available from biblehub.com

[120] Ibid.

heart) of the scribes and Pharisees is filthy, and the tithe was paid to clean the outside of the cup, we can therefore deduce that the purpose of the tithe was for the window-dressing of the heart (the inside of the cup). It was to cover up for their excesses. The same may be true for Christians who practice tithing.

Point 9 (Matthew 23:26):

✓ **Pureness of heart will deliver you from the bondage of tithing.**

Matthew 23:26 (KJV)

[26] Thou blind Pharisee, cleanse first that which is within the cup and platter, that the outside of them may be clean also.

Even though the Pharisees were the official interpreters of the Law of Moses (Matthew 23:2), yet Jesus addressed them in Matthew 23:26 as *blind fellows*. And truly they were. Just like their name may suggest, the "Pharisees" were "far to see" the things of the Spirit. They were "far to see" that they were not doing things in the proper way, and this seemed not to have bothered them at all because of their spiritual blindness. Jesus, knowing who the Pharisees were, had warned the crowd that had gathered around him, not to follow the hypocritical ways of the Pharisees; whatever they do is merely for a show and not for religious piety (Matthew 23:3-5). So, fully aware of their spiritual blindness and show of spirituality, Jesus admonished both the scribes and Pharisees in Matthew 23:26 to clean the inside of the cup (a symbol of *the heart*). Only by so-doing will render the outside of the cup clean.

Note that regarding the cleaning of the cup, Jesus only pointed at one space of the cup: *the inside*. He didn't say that the scribes and Pharisees had to clean the outside of the cup, which he saw as unnecessary. The cleaning of the inside of the cup will automatically make its outside clean. When the heart of the believer is pure, his whole body will be pure. Seek God with your whole heart, and not your flesh. Tithe is of the flesh. Justice, mercy, and faith are of the heart. This was the message Jesus was sending across to the Jews in a figurative language.

Remember that one of the reasons why Jesus always used parables when speaking to the scribes and Pharisees was because he didn't want to be apprehended by them for breaking their law, in this case the law of tithing. He was so conscious of his earthly assignment. He didn't want his ministry to be brought to a premature end.

2. LUKE

Point 1 (Luke 18:10-13):

✓ **Your tithe does not lead you to God.**

Point 2 (Luke 18:10-13):

✓ **Tithe bestows pseudo spirituality.**

Luke 18:10-13 (NLT)

[10] "Two men went up to the temple to pray. One was a Pharisee, and the other was a despised tax collector.

[11] The Pharisee stood by himself and prayed this prayer: 'I thank you, God, that I am not a sinner like everyone else. For I don't cheat, I don't sin, and I don't commit adultery. I'm certainly not like that tax collector!

[12] I fast twice a week, and I give you a tenth of my income.'

[13] "But the tax collector stood at a distance and dared not even lift his eyes to heaven, but beat his breast and said, 'God, have mercy on me, a sinner.'

We can all see that due to the works of the law, the Pharisee had grown so big to the extent that he had become a judge pointing out the sins of others. Had it been the Pharisee had not given his tithes, he wouldn't have been emboldened the way he was. Verse 11 says this about the Pharisee: He "stood and prayed thus with himself." So, the prayer of the Pharisee, the man *who gave tithes of all that he possessed*, did not ascend into the heavens for he was only praying with himself, and not to God. The bigger problem here for the Pharisee, and for all those who practice tithing and even make a boast of it in their heart, is this: the tithe giver is probably not aware of the fact that their tithe-linked prayers are not heard in heaven, like the case of this Pharisee. The Pharisee left the temple ground with a pseudo assurance in his heart that he had prayed to God, telling God all the good things he, the Pharisee, had done and assuring himself that the Lord was so proud of him. But that was not the case as revealed in verse 14. So, the Pharisee's practice of tithing, which emboldened him and imparted him with self-righteousness, made him miss God.

The publican, on the other hand, recognized he was a sinner. This was something that the Pharisee never did. We do understand now better why Jesus, in Matthew 23:23, described the Pharisees as blind men. The publican stood quite a distance away because he knew that neither the tithe nor any component of the law could save him. He relied solely on what would save him from his sinful state: the MERCY of God. And, remember, 'mercy' is one of the "weightier matters of the law" that Jesus pointed out to the scribes and Pharisees in Matthew 23:23 stated here-above.

Point 3 (Luke 18:14):

✓   Your tithes cannot justify your salvation.

Luke 18:14 (NLT)

14 "I tell you, this sinner, not the Pharisee, returned home justified before God. For those who exalt themselves will be humbled, and those who humble themselves will be exalted."

Finally, the publican, who had been castigated by the self-righteous-tithe-paying Pharisee for not practicing the law as the latter did, was justified for salvation meanwhile the keeper of the law was not. This is a clear message from our Lord Jesus Christ: Your tithes cannot justify your salvation. Only the mercy of God can. Take it or leave it.

3. EPHESIANS

Ephesians 2:8

8 For it is by grace you have been saved, through faith—and this is not from yourselves, it is the gift of God—

Point 1 (Ephesians 2:8):

✓   Tithing is not an act of faith; So, it is sinful.

Point 2 (Ephesians 2:8):

✓   Tithing does not depend on grace; So, it cannot save.

Chapter 2 of Ephesians tells us that only by grace are we saved, which comes through our faith in Christ. And faith is "the correct application of the Word of God in the life of the believer." Simply applying God's Word in one's life doesn't make it an act of faith. If that were so, then the slaughtering of a goat in a church service for the atonement of the sins of the congregation could be said to be an act of faith. But such a practice cannot be likened to an act of faith for a church because it is not consistent with the demands of the new covenant under which the Church, in general, finds herself. In other words, performing in a church service what we have just described here above is a wrong application of the Word of God. It can only be qualified as a taboo as far as the New Testament Church is concerned.

Tithing can be said to be an act of faith for the Jew, not for the Christian. And because it is not an act of faith for the Christian, its indulgence is sinful for "whatsoever is not of faith is sin (Romans 14:23)." In addition, no one can please God without faith (Hebrews 11:6). Since tithing is not an act of faith for the Christian and taking into consideration Hebrews 11:6, it can be concluded that the Christian tithe-giver cannot please God based on their practice of tithing.

It is for the above reasons that tithing cannot stand as a doctrine for the New Testament Church for it contradicts the principle of the gospel of salvation by grace through faith. It contradicts this principle in the sense that:

(1) it is not an act of faith for it is derived from a wrong interpretation of the Scripture with regards to the Church and

(2) it does not depend on the work of GRACE in man; rather, it depends on the work of man in the Law. That is the difference!

This grace we are talking about is a gift of God. It is not under the control of the believer. The believer cannot adjust or change the way it should operate in their life. It is a divine prerogative of God's Son, the Lord Jesus Christ. The tithe, on the other hand, is under the control of the believer. They can choose how much, where, when, and how often to pay it. Unlike GRACE, tithe is the work of the flesh, and the sinful flesh cannot save anything. And because tithing is the work of the flesh, it is impossible for the sinful flesh not to boast of the latter's achievement.

Point 3 (Ephesians 2:9):

✓ **The believer who practices tithing is boastful by default.**

Ephesians 2:9 (NLT)

⁹ Salvation is not a reward for the good things we have done, so none of us can boast about it.

As the passage above clearly puts it, because tithing is the work of the flesh, anyone who practices it is boastful by default, the humility trait of the person concerned notwithstanding.

A bird that stands on the branch of a tree is not afraid of the branch breaking off the tree because its trust is not in the branch but in its own ability to fly off. A man, on the other hand, holding the branch of a tree has zero trust in himself in the event of an emergency. The reason is because the man in question is conscious of his lack of ability to save himself from falling onto the ground. His trust lies only in the ability of God to prevent the branch from breaking off or to create some miraculous shock absorber on the ground below him for safe landing.

The bird in the illustration above could be likened to a tithe payer. In order to be saved from sin (the branch break), the tithe payer puts his trust in what he can do rather than in what God will do. He sees his ability to tithe as a saving (messianic) force that would bail him out of any predicament.

Point 4 (Ephesians 2:10):

✓ **We, not tithes, are the workmanship of God.**

Ephesians 2:10 (KJV)

¹⁰ For we are his workmanship, created in Christ Jesus unto good works, which God hath before ordained that we should walk in them.

After Apostle Paul had explained in Ephesians 2:9 that none should boast for none will be saved by the works of the law they practice, he went further to elaborate in Ephesians 2:10 why we will be saved only by God's grace. It is because we are God's work of art, or workmanship, as KJV puts it."

The term "workmanship" is used in seven different places in the Scripture (Exodus 31:3, 5; 35:31; 2 Kings 16:10; 1 Chronicles 28:21; Ezekiel 28:13, and Ephesians 2:10) and it seems to reflect the special work of God in our creation. Consider Exodus 31:1-3 and Ezekiel 28:13 stated here-below:

Exodus 31:1-3 (KJV)

¹ And the LORD spake unto Moses, saying,

² "See, I have called by name Bezaleel the son of Uri, the son of Hur, of the tribe of Judah:

³ And I have filled him with the spirit of God, in wisdom, and in understanding, and in knowledge, and in all manner of **workmanship.**

Ezekiel 28:13 (KJV)

¹³ Thou hast been in Eden, the garden of God; every precious stone was thy covering, the sardius, topaz, and the diamond, the beryl, the onyx, and the jasper, the sapphire, the emerald, and the carbuncle, and gold: the **workmanship** of thy tabrets and of thy pipes was prepared in thee in the day that thou wast created.

Therefore, by making allusion of the fact that we are the workmanship of God, the writer of Ephesians is saying that since our creation and election come from God, it therefore follows that our salvation likewise comes from Him. So, to merit their salvation, the believer should look up to their Maker, not to their ability to tithe.

In Ephesians 2:10, following the expression, "For we are his workmanship" is the clause "created in Christ Jesus unto good works, which God hath before ordained that we should walk in them." The believer of Christ is created in Christ to do the good works which Christ had spoken of in the Scripture. In other words, to continue in the good works that Christ began in us. The 'good works' are clearly defined here as those works that have been divinely ordained in advance for Christian practice. And they can be found in the Gospel. These are the works and teachings of Christ. Looking at the life and teachings of Christ, Jesus never practiced tithing nor taught any of his followers to tithe. The same observation is true with his immediate followers, the Twelve Apostles.

Now, you may want to ask, "Why do most church leaders compel members of their congregation to practice tithing?" The answer is simple, "Greed!" To satisfy their greed for materialistic wealth, pro-tithe church leaders have employed the secular tools of manipulation to deceive the ignorant and gullible members of their congregation to surrender into the offering basket of the local church 10% of their income.

Since neither Christ nor his disciples did practice or teach tithing to their followers, tithing cannot be taken today to constitute a church doctrine. It is for this reason that we strongly hold that the practice of tithing in the New Testament Church is nothing but a manipulation aimed at fulfilling the selfish desires of the church leader.

4. COLOSSIANS

Point 1 (Colossians 2:10):

> ✓ **You do not need to pay tithes to be complete in Christ.**

Colossians 2:10

[10] and in Christ you have been brought to fullness. He is the head over every power and authority.

The believer of Christ is complete in Christ without the practice of tithing, in particular, or the works of the law, in general. This is because tithing does not constitute a part of the message of the gospel ('the Good News').

Moses came with the Law. Christ came with the gospel. The Law was given to Moses and his followers to be practiced in a bid to achieve their salvation. The gospel, on the other hand, was given to Christ and his followers for the same purpose, that is, for achieving one's salvation. To achieve their salvation, the followers of Moses were required to practice every component of the Law meanwhile the followers of Christ simply have to lean on their master, Christ Jesus, who had fulfilled the entire Law on their behalf through his death on the cross.

Followers of Moses are incomplete in the eyes of God without the works of the Law. Followers of Christ, on the other hand, are complete in God's eyes by virtue of their faith in Christ who had quenched the wrath of God through his death. The follower of Christ, therefore, does not need to tithe or practice the Law to be complete in Christ. It is for this reason that tithing, or the Law, in general, cannot be regarded as a qualification for 'spiritual completeness' in matters relating to one's salvation as far as the Christian faith is concerned.

The simple message of the gospel that "ye are complete in him" through faith in him is true for Christ is, Colossians 2:10 continues, "the head of all principality and power." Christ is not a man that he should lie. You have to listen to him and his faithful disciples. You do not need to listen to the deception of the compromised whose sole interest is to drain you of your finances and make themselves rich at the expense of the gospel.

Point 2 (Colossians 2:11-13):

> ✓ **The Priesthood of All Believers abolishes tithing.**

Colossians 2:11-13

[11] In him you were also circumcised with a circumcision not performed by human hands. Your whole self ruled by the flesh was put off when you were circumcised by Christ,

[12] having been buried with him in baptism, in which you were also raised with him through your faith in the working of God, who raised him from the dead.

[13] When you were dead in your sins and in the uncircumcision of your flesh, God made you alive with Christ. He forgave us all our sins,

Circumcision was required for the Jew to be considered a part of God's family. God told Abraham to circumcise all the males in his household including the bondservants. In the first century Church, dominated by Jewish Christians, some of the Jewish believers required that the Gentiles be circumcised before they could be admitted into their fellowship. Paul, in this passage, was telling the Colossians that they do not need to perform the law of circumcision to be followers of Christ for anyone who confesses their belief in the Messiah and resolves to follow him is already circumcised in Christ. The circumcision of the follower of Christ is of the heart, not of the flesh.

Colossians 2:11 gives us a revelation of what the original purpose of circumcision, as practiced by the Jews, was supposed to be: "to put off the body of the sins of the flesh." The New Testament, which is the revelation of the Old Testament, looks at the root or original purpose of the Law. Since the law of circumcision was aimed at "putting off the body of the sins of the flesh," and given that the believer's sins are "buried with Christ in baptism" (Colossians 2:12), performing a physical circumcision is, therefore, not required.

Even though you were dead in your sins by reason of the uncircumcision of your flesh, Colossians 2:13 continues, Christ has forgiven all your sins, and has brought you back to life by reason of your faith in him. Therefore, you do not need to be circumcised anymore for your sins have all been forgiven.

The same is true for tithing, and of the Law, in general. Note that in the old covenant, the Levites were chosen to constitute the priesthood for the entire nation of Israel. To dedicate themselves in the work of the Temple, they were forbidden from owning any personal properties. As a result, the law of tithing was created. The non-Levitical tribes were commanded by God to bring a tenth of their cultivated crops and cattle to the Levites. This was the original purpose of tithing. Today, the Levitical Priesthood has been replaced by the Priesthood of Christ whereby Christ is the High Priest, and his followers are all priests (the Priesthood of All Believers).

Like in the case of circumcision explained here-above, there is, therefore, no necessity for the believer in Christ to give to another believer 10% of their cultivated crops or cattle for they are all priests, and none has been forbidden from acquiring personal properties. This accounts for the reason why the practice of tithing in the Church is repugnant to the gospel message.

Point 3 (Colossians 2:14-15):

✓   **Tithing has been nailed to the cross.**

Colossians 2:14-15

[14] having canceled the charge of our legal indebtedness, which stood against us and condemned us; he has taken it away, nailing it to the cross.

[15] And having disarmed the powers and authorities, he made a public spectacle of them, triumphing over them by the cross.

The law has always stood in the way between God and Man. By condemning Man, the law made it pretty difficult for Man to approach his Maker. This was the reason for which God's Son was sent to this world. When Christ came, he "blotted out the handwriting of the ordinances that was against us" and nailed it to his cross. Tithing is one of those ordinances that have been nailed to the cross of our Savior. It is for this reason that the Church of Christ is no more required to practice the law of tithing for tithing has been crucified on the cross at Calvary. Doing such knowingly or unknowingly is making mockery of the finished work of Christ. Such an action can only be qualified as an abomination.

It is sad to say that even though Christ has taken the handwriting of the Law out of the way, the handwriting of the ordinance of tithing, to be specific, is still printed in the hearts of some Christian believers today. And this is largely due to ignorance of the truth. However, ignorance of the content of a law is never an excuse before a sitting judge.

Point 4 (Colossians 2:16-18):

> ✓ **The believer of Christ is not judged by their tithes.**

Colossians 2:16-18

16 Therefore do not let anyone judge you by what you eat or drink, or with regard to a religious festival, a New Moon celebration or a Sabbath day.

17 These are a shadow of the things that were to come; the reality, however, is found in Christ.

18 Do not let anyone who delights in false humility and the worship of angels disqualify you. Such a person also goes into great detail about what they have seen; they are puffed up with idle notions by their unspiritual mind.

Let no man judge you in meat, drink, holyday, the new moon, or the Sabbath. And the list goes on and on. These are all elements of the Law. The Jews lived a life of strict obedience to these laws. They ate only the meat the Law permitted them to eat. They were judged and rewarded according to their level of obedience to the Law. For the follower of Christ, it is not so! They will not be judged by the food they eat or the tithing they practice. What this means is that these things are inconsequential with respect to the believer's salvation. Faith in Christ is enough!

Tithing as a Measuring Rod for Faithfulness

Unfortunately, today, tithing is being used as a yardstick in many churches to judge if a member is a faithful and committed Christian or not. I have personally seen a situation where a church member was appointed an elder based on the size of his tithes. In some churches, a member cannot approach the church authorities for any financial or moral assistance if they are not established tithe payers. It is horrible.

5. HEBREWS

Point 1 (Hebrews 7:11-12):

> ✓ **Your tithes cannot bring you into a union with God.**

Hebrews 7:11-12

11 If perfection could have been attained through the Levitical priesthood—and indeed the law given to the people established that priesthood—why was there still need for another priest to come, one in the order of Melchizedek, not in the order of Aaron?

¹² For when the priesthood is changed, the law must be changed also.

Since the Levitical Priesthood was an imperfect system, with its laws unable to bring men into a perfect union with God, God saw it necessary to raise another priest, His own Son. A change of the priesthood required a change of the laws. They that believe in God's Son, Jesus Christ, are no more going to practice the law of tithing (which was attached to the old priesthood) as a requirement for their justification. All they have to do is put their faith in Christ Jesus, and walk their Christian journey according to his teachings as found in the gospel.

Point 2 (Hebrews 7:13-14):

✓ Pastors have no mandate to collect tithes.

Hebrews 7:13-14

¹³ He of whom these things are said belonged to a different tribe, and no one from that tribe has ever served at the altar.

¹⁴ For it is clear that our Lord descended from Judah, and in regard to that tribe Moses said nothing about priests.

According to the Law of Moses, it must be recalled, only the Jews who came from the tribe of Levi were mandated to collect tithes from their fellow non-Levitical Jews. Since Jesus was not from that tribe, he could not collect tithes. If Christ, the head of the Church, did not collect tithes from anyone during his earthly ministry, it would be a betrayal and a desecration of the message of the Gospel of Christ for a church leader, who is presumed to be a servant of Christ, to collect tithes from anyone, whether they are Christians or not.

Point 3 (Hebrews 8:6-7):

✓ Christian tithing is a misfaith.

Hebrews 8:6-7

⁶ But in fact the ministry Jesus has received is as superior to theirs as the covenant of which he is mediator is superior to the old one, since the new covenant is established on better promises.

⁷ For if there had been nothing wrong with that first covenant, no place would have been sought for another.

Our Lord Jesus Christ is the mediator of a better covenant, the new covenant. This is the covenant of Grace where we are saved not by the works of the Law, as was the case with the old covenant, but by the works of Christ in us, which were fulfilled by Christ's death on the cross. Since followers of Christ are under the new covenant in which Christ is the covenant mediator, and since tithing does not belong to this covenant, it is a "misfaith," that is, a misplacement of faith for followers of Christ to practice tithing.

Point 4 (Hebrews 8:12-13):

> ✓ **The new covenant makes tithing obsolete.**

Hebrews 8:12-13

[12] For I will forgive their wickedness and will remember their sins no more."

[13] By calling this covenant "new," he has made the first one obsolete; and what is obsolete and outdated will soon disappear.

The blood of Jesus Christ, the mediator of the new covenant, has now done that which the old covenant, through the works of the law, could not do. By shedding his blood on the cross, the mediator of the better covenant has satisfied the wrath of God. The Lord Most High will remember the iniquities of His people no more. He will be merciful to them. Practicing the laws of the old covenant is, therefore, not necessary as the wrath of God has already been appeased. The old covenant has now vanished away together with its laws.

Israel's Failure to be "A Kingdom of Priests" Paved the Way for Tithing

Tithing wouldn't have existed in the first place if the children of Israel had not sinned by worshiping the golden calf, Kelly argues. Kelly goes further to elaborate the sequence of events that would have occurred.

One: Israel would have become a "kingdom of priests," fulfilling Exodus 19:5-6.

Two: If all were priests, the land would have been distributed to every tribe, eliminating the need to offer tithes to those who do not have lands, as was the case with the Levites.

Three: Since there were priests everywhere to assist Aaron and his sons, no one would be required to travel from a distance far enough to require any sustenance from tithes.

Four: The ordinance of tithing in Numbers 18 would not have been given.

Five: The servant duties performed by the Levites would have been shouldered by all priests.

Six: Freewill offerings and the temple shekel would have provided sufficient funds.

A Final Word to this Section

Nehemiah 8:12

[12] Then all the people went away to eat and drink, to send portions of food and to celebrate with great joy, because they now understood the words that had been made known to them.

We have come to the end of our biblical analysis of the ordinance of tithing. Just like the people of Israel, who had been grieved for disobeying God due to their ignorance of God's Word (Nehemiah 8:11), returned to God after coming to understand properly what was written in the Book, we believe that the revelation you have gotten from the biblical exposition of tithing above will reshape your walk with God.

You may be asking yourself this question, "If this is the blatant biblical truth about tithing, why then are most pastors that I know not speaking up and rebuking others who preach tithing?" Good question. The answer is simple. Most pastors will not rebuke the practice of tithing in the church. This is because if they do, they will be shooting themselves on the foot. That is to say, if they denounce the practice of tithing, they, too, will not receive the tithe money from their own congregation. And that is the least thing they are prepared to do.

I was shocked when I listened to a preacher whom I had once admired for his outspokenness on tithing twist the talk when he said, "Even though tithing is not a Christian doctrine, you can still pay your tithes into your local church if you know they're using the money to help the poor." Guess why this preacher said this. He, too, was collecting tithes from members of his congregation. This is what we call 'compromising the Word of God.'

MANIPULATIONS IN TITHING

1 John 2:26-27

[26] "I am writing these things to you about those who are trying to lead you astray.

[27] As for you, the anointing you received from him remains in you, and you do not need anyone to teach you. But as his anointing teaches you about all things and as that anointing is real, not counterfeit—just as it has taught you, remain in him."

In the next pages, we are going to reveal some of the most efficient tools that have been employed by preachers to seduce Christians to tithe.

TOOLS OF MANIPULATION IN TITHING

<u>Manipulation #1:</u>

Tithing Rebrand

Acts 13:10

[10] "You are a child of the devil and an enemy of everything that is right! You are full of all kinds of deceit and trickery. Will you never stop perverting the right ways of the Lord?"

The first strategy employed by tithe-collecting church leaders is the rebranding of tithing as explained in the following steps:

(1) They have removed tithing from the list of laws enshrined in the Law of Moses. They have done so because they know that as part of the Law tithing has no place in the New Testament Church according to the writings of Paul,

(2) They have re-branded tithing and called it simply "giving." The re-branding of tithing was meant to ease the consciences. This is similar to a bandit who has to consume some drugs to kill their conscience so that they will have no remorse when carrying out their criminal operations. The church leaders go further to teach members of their congregation that the re-branded law of tithing brings blessings to those who obey it. They do this for the sake of collecting 10% of the income of their church members. To increase their financial power, they have made the payment of tithes compulsory to the believers in their congregation. These church leaders have become like the Jewish believers in Acts 15:5 who belonged to the sect of the Pharisees and who all stood up and boldly declared: "The Gentile converts must be circumcised and required to follow the Law of Moses (NIV)." A number of the apostles in the church at Jerusalem rebuked the Pharisee believers beginning with Peter (vv. 7-11) who said (vv. 10): "Why tempt ye God, to put a yoke upon the neck of the disciples, which neither our fathers nor we were able to bear?" Peter then concluded (vv. 11): "But we believe that through the grace of the Lord Jesus Christ we shall be saved, even as they." Peter's discourse was immediately followed by that of Barnabas, Paul, and James (vv. 12ff). It is evident from the above passages that anyone who requires more than God for their salvation is *challenging God* or *testing God's Holy Spirit.*

(3) They have associated tithing with freewill offerings. That's why you

will hear them say, "Now is the time to collect our tithes and offerings." Tithing is not "giving" because it is not freewill, Wells writes. [121] The New Testament endorses freewill offerings but NEVER does it endorse tithing.

Manipulation #2:

Tithing is a Prerequisite for Divine Blessing

Jeremiah 8:10

[10] Therefore I will give their wives to other men and their fields to new owners. From the least to the greatest, all are greedy for gain; prophets and priests alike, all practice deceit.

Through preaching, ministers of the gospel have deceived their congregation that to be blessed or favored by God, the congregation must first ensure that their tithes are paid. God will not listen to the plea of a non-tither, they claim. And some of the folks actually believe this lie.

I had a telephone conversation on tithing with a pastor friend of mine. After having explained to him with some scriptural passages why tithing in the Church is wrong, he boldly told me that regardless of all what I had said, he still believed in tithing and was going to keep on tithing because it was due to his faithfulness in tithing that God kept blessing him. Toward the end of our discussion, this pastor friend confessed to me that his wife had been seriously sick for the past seven months, and that they had been busy looking for where to borrow money in order to book a surgical appointment to no avail. In addition, he opened up to me that he had not paid his rents for the last three months. I later discovered that his monthly rent was even higher than his monthly salary. I could not believe my eyes. When I asked him why? His reply was, "I live by faith." I was so furious in my spirit, but not wanting to compound his problems, I said within myself, "You're living by foolishness for living in an apartment whose monthly rent is greater than your monthly earning." The Scripture clearly makes mention of "the curse of the law" for anyone who practices the law. This might have probably been the case for my dear pastor friend. He kept on practicing tithing yet he was languishing in poverty while at the same time living a life of indiscretion. Such a lifestyle is not befitting to a child in the kingdom of God who lives a simple life of faith in Christ.

Church leaders, to continue, tell their congregation that tithing will be the solution to their problems when the exact opposite is true by virtue

---

[121] Wells, *The Great Tithing Debate*, 3.

of an objective biblical analysis of tithing – the main task of this book. Tithing takes the believer back to the Law, which is the source of all the problems and curses humanity faces today. How foolish are we to think that we will attract God's blessings and eventually obtain our salvation by fulfilling only one out of the six hundred and thirteen (613) laws that were given under the old covenant whereas the Giver of the Law Himself required a perfect obedience of the Law for the reward of one's blessings and salvation (Deuteronomy 26:16-19)? In the days of old, no one could; today, still no one can. That was the reason why Jesus had to come down here on earth to do it for us, and he actually did it once and for ALL (Matthew 5:17), having nailed all of the laws to his cross (Colossians 2:14).

If you really do believe that tithing "will open the windows of heaven" for you, or that any success you've seen this far came your way as a result of your act or practice of tithing, know you've been deceived. If you believe you're "robbing God" or are "under a curse" for not tithing, then know you've been deceived intentionally or otherwise. Whatever be the case, you've been deceived. The truth is that, you who tithe and your pastor who tells you to do so are the true robbers of God. However, you are not robbing God of any material resources; you are robbing God of His new covenant plan of grace in your life, a covenant for which He sacrificed the precious blood of His only begotten Son, Jesus Christ. You are robbing God when you replace His covenant of grace, the covenant that finally satisfied God's wrath, with the one that kept God's wrath alive – the Law.

<u>Manipulation #3:</u>

Tithe as Financial Insurance

Romans 3:13

[13] "Their throats are open graves; their tongues practice deceit. The poison of vipers is on their lips."

Christians are deceived into thinking that tithing constitutes an insurance scheme for their assets. They are told that if they give to God ten percent (a tithe) of their possessions, God will not only receive with gladness the tithe and multiply it, but He will also sanctify and multiply the remaining ninety percent that's in their keeping. That is, the giving of the tithe sanctifies the remaining ninety percent. And to this they add, "God is a generous God."

You will hear all sort of motivational statements like, "God will anoint the natural to produce the supernatural" and "If you do not tithe, things will be tight for you," just to mention these two. And hearing such words of deception puts those believers in the congregation who do not tithe into a state of fear and panic. They will then have no option but to enter into an "insurance arrangement with God" by forfeiting 10% of their possessions and continue to obey the rule strictly over the rest of their lives.

The manipulated believer is like a driver whose car has been properly insured yet drives with utmost fear as if their car has no insurance cover. The fear of the unknown drives them to their local pastor to surrender 10% of their income. So sad!

Manipulation #4:

Fear Instigation

Romans 16:17-18

[17] I urge you, brothers and sisters, to watch out for those who cause divisions and put obstacles in your way that are contrary to the teaching you have learned. Keep away from them.

[18] For such people are not serving our Lord Christ, but their own appetites. By smooth talk and flattery they deceive the minds of naive people.

One of the principal ways through which most pastors manipulate their congregation into paying tithes is by instilling enormous fear in them. Their scriptural base for this is Malachi 3:9. The author of this book you're reading now has once been a victim for a very long time. Some would refer to the tithe as "the Holy Seed." It is not uncommon to hear tithe-collecting pastors say, "Please, do not touch the tithe else God becomes angry with you. The tithe is God's sacred portion. It is meant for Him alone. If you eat it, you'll attract a curse in your life."

Regarding the issue of tithing in the Church, Let Us Reason Ministries writes:

"Why are we taught that we should no longer be doing animal sacrifice today but we should still be tithing? The Law of Moses was a unit that cannot be divided, either we keep it all which brings us out from the new covenant or we separate from it all and keep the new covenant. If we are to be cursed for not keeping a certain portion of the Law of Moses, then we are cursed for not keeping the other 613 laws included in the Law." [122]

---

[122] *The Origin of Tithing*, Internet; accessed 28 December 2017; available from http://www.letusreason.org/doct54.htm

How Can Grace Be Free?

Under the covenant of GRACE, we are given everything for free. It is difficult for advocates of tithing to imagine how this can be so because according to the reasoning pattern of the world, nothing is free. Tithe advocates are simply blinded by the works of the law they practice (2 Corinthians 3:14). I guess that is why followers of Christ are prohibited from being conformed to the reasoning pattern of this world but to renew their minds through the Scripture. Don't, as a bid to earn your salvation, try to overshoot heaven with works that aren't required.

These church leaders fail to understand that by compelling members of their congregation to tithe, they are simply bringing them under 'the curse of the law.'

In a church service, a pastor told the congregation that his multi-millionaire friend doesn't tithe, and that if that friend of his doesn't begin paying his tithes as soon as possible, the wings of his private jet were going to rust off. And the whole congregation burst into laughter without ever stopping to think that the guy they were making mockery of became a multi-millionaire without a single act of tithing. [123]

Pastors Will Fight You for Stopping Them from Collecting Tithes

The manipulation and enjoyment of 'the tithe money' have eaten ministers of the gospel so deep that when you call them to order, do not be surprised if you are labeled as 'unspiritual' or even a heretic. This was the same with Martin Luther. When Luther taught that salvation comes from grace alone, and not from the performance of ordinances or church-related requirements, he was branded a heretic and subsequently programmed for elimination. Why were the church leaders bent on eliminating Luther? They could not imagine the amount of money they were going to lose if the believers were to be enlightened by the truth of the gospel, which Luther was going to spread across.

Let's consider the case of Jesus, the Head of the Church. He was also branded a heretic by the Pharisees not because he was one but simply because he tampered with the Jewish religious system. Like leaders of church institutions, the Pharisees did that to Jesus because they were not prepared to lose their fame and the money they made from the system they had put in place.

---

[123] Wells, *The Great Tithing Debate*, 3.

There is a lot of conspiracy, Bruce Wells writes, that has been built around the practice of tithing in the Church to the extent that when you don't tithe or dare to question the legitimacy of tithing, you will be made to feel that you're under God's judgment. [124] But God welcomes all sorts of questions for He has answers to all our questions. If God really wanted the Church to tithe, He would have told us explicitly through His written Word.

Manipulation #5:

You Are Robbing God!

Ezekiel 34:4

[4] You have not strengthened the weak or healed the sick or bound up the injured. You have not brought back the strays or searched for the lost. You have ruled them harshly and brutally.

A very successful tool most preachers use to get those in their congregation who do not tithe to do so is by systematically implanting in them the guilt that they are robbing God if they fail to bring to God 'His tithe.' It is commonly said that "there is power in repetition." As the preacher constantly utters this robbing-God accusation, guilt begins to build itself up in the non-tither little by little, and, before you know it, the person concerned begins to feel guilty of a crime they never committed; a supposed crime whose guilt they would never had felt, ceteris paribus. And this is exactly the same way secular advertisements work. On your TV screen, a product is advertised a number of times for as short as three to five seconds per slot. The potential buyer does not really feel the impact of a single slot. However, as they are exposed to a series of slots, they become chained or hooked up in the propaganda agenda of the advertiser's advertisement, which leads them to the advertiser's shop for purchase.

Among tithe-collecting pastors, it is difficult to find a single person who does not use this tool of manipulation. It is an anthem in their mouth in clamping down on believers who do not dance to their "pay-your-tithes" tune.

The Famous cliché:
When Last Did You Pay Your Tithe?

When members are sick or in need of a breakthrough and turn to their

---

[124] Wells, *The Great Tithing Debate*, 8.

pastor for prayers or financial support, some of the pastors would first ask, "When last did you pay your tithe?" When the answer is, "I have not been paying for a while," the pastor, quoting Malachi 3:8-10, immediately identifies the member's non-payment of tithe as the root cause of their problem. Do we need to pay God in order to receive His blessings? The gospel of Jesus Christ has been monetized to an alarming proportion.

Let Us Reason Ministries writes:

> "No Christian should be coerced into giving a set amount to receive God's blessings. The simple reason is that it removes them from walking in grace and puts them under the law. You will always find that those who promote the 'give to get concept' will use the Old Testament. They will interpret the new in light of the old, not the old in light of the new." [125]

After reading in an article the statistics of tithe payment among evangelicals in America, R.C. Sproul, founding pastor of Saint Andrew's Chapel, Sanford, Fla. (USA), applies the same accusation, as shown here-below:

> "Recently, I read an article that gave an astonishing statistic that I find difficult to believe is accurate. It declared that of all of the people in America who identify themselves as evangelical Christians, only four percent of them return a tithe to God. If that statistic is accurate, it means that ninety-six percent of professing evangelical Christians regularly, systematically, habitually, and impenitently rob God of what belongs to Him. It also means that ninety-six percent of us are for this reason exposing ourselves to a divine curse upon our lives. Whether this percentage is accurate, one thing is certain – it is clear that the overwhelming majority of professing evangelical Christians do not tithe."[126]

Billy Graham attributes the loss of one's money to non-tithing:

> "We are so guilty of the sin of covetousness that we actually rob God of that which belongs to Him. Millions may be lost because Christians were too covetous to give that which belongs to God. The Scripture warns in Habakkuk 2:9, 'Woe to him who covets.'"[127]

"The threat of 'robbing God' puts people in a state of fear," Christopher Johnson writes. "Once in a state of fear," he continues, "pastors tell them to open their wallets, and give everything they can, even to 'give until it hurts' as they often say in our modern day."[128]

---

[125] *The Origin of Tithing*, Internet; accessed 28 December 2017; available from http://www.letusreason.org/doct54.htm.

[126] R.C. Sproul, *Will Man Rob God?* Internet; accessed 26 July 2020; available from https://www.ligonier.org/learn/articles/will-man-rob-god/.

[127] Billy Graham, *Are You Robbing God?* Internet; accessed 29 July 2020; available from https://decisionmagazine.com/are-you-robbing-god/.

[128] Christopher J. E. Johnson, *Tithe Is Not a Christian Requirement*; Internet; accessed 26 July 2020; available from http://www.creationliberty.com/articles/tithe.php.

However, if we look at it critically, the pastors who employ this manipulative tool are actually the ones who are robbing the ignorant members of their congregation. They do not only rob the believers of their material resources, but they also do rob them of the truth in the Word of God. And most of these pastors know this very well, but, unfortunately, the love of money has held them captive.

Jesus Warned:

Feed the Sheep! Do Not Exploit Them!

The feeding of the sheep is a key preoccupation in the ministry of Jesus. Remember what Jesus told Peter. And it was so important to Jesus that he repeated the same request three times to the annoyance of Peter:

John 21:15-17

15 When they had finished eating, Jesus said to Simon Peter, "Simon son of John, do you love me more than these?" "Yes, Lord," he said, "you know that I love you." Jesus said, "Feed my lambs."

16 Again Jesus said, "Simon son of John, do you love me?" He answered, "Yes, Lord, you know that I love you." Jesus said, "Take care of my sheep."

17 The third time he said to him, "Simon son of John, do you love me?" Peter was hurt because Jesus asked him the third time, "Do you love me?" He said, "Lord, you know all things; you know that I love you." Jesus said, "Feed my sheep.

On the same note 1 Peter 5:2-4 cautions:

1 Peter 5:2-4

2 Be shepherds of God's flock that is under your care, watching over them—not because you must, but because you are willing, as God wants you to be; not pursuing dishonest gain, but eager to serve;

3 not lording it over those entrusted to you, but being examples to the flock.

4 And when the Chief Shepherd appears, you will receive the crown of glory that will never fade away.

Manipulation #6:

Greed Holds Back Your Blessings

Jeremiah 5:27

27 Like cages full of birds, their houses are full of deceit; they have become rich and powerful.

To compel non-tithers to succumb to tithing, the tithe-collecting pastors tell the congregation that there is a spiritual financial warfare in tithing, which is caused by greed. They now go on to instigate fear in non-tithers by saying that greed is one of the seven deadly sins. Greed, they continue, is Satan's economic tool to prevent Christians from tithing, and thereby robbing them of the blessings attached to tithing.

<u>Manipulation #7:</u>

Tithe to be a Full Church Member

1 Timothy 4:1-2

[1] The Spirit clearly says that in later times some will abandon the faith and follow deceiving spirits and things taught by demons.

[2] Such teachings come through hypocritical liars, whose consciences have been seared as with a hot iron.

The church institution deserves most of the criticism it receives from the world. The criticism comes because of the poor manner in which the Church, the supposedly "Heaven's Ambassador to the world," has represented Heaven so far. The world, which has been looking up to the Church for spiritual guidance, has finally come to the realization that the Church isn't doing what she had been appointed to do. If the status quo of church institutions doesn't change, we can't really blame the world for the firm stance it has taken vis-à-vis the Church in general. For the world to change its perception regarding the Church, it is incumbent upon church institutions to change the way they operate by sticking to the biblical truth as expressed in the gospel. To quote Bruce Wells, "Those who hate the church would probably love it if they could find the 'real' Jesus." [129]

Gentiles Denied Church Membership Due to Non-Circumcision

In the same way some churches today have made the payment of tithes a requirement for church membership, during the time of the Apostles, some of the Jewish followers of Christ had forbidden their Gentile counterparts from becoming members of the community of Christ's followers based on the fact that the Gentiles had not been circumcised. The Gentiles were told they would be admitted only under one condition: be circumcised.

---

[129] Wells, *The Great Tithing Debate*, 12.

Acts 15:5-6

⁵ Then some of the believers who belonged to the party of the Pharisees stood up and said, "The Gentiles must be circumcised and required to keep the law of Moses."

⁶ The apostles and elders met to consider this question.

After Apostle Peter had learned of this, he did intervene, as shown below:

Acts 15:7-11

⁷ After much discussion, Peter got up and addressed them: "Brothers, you know that some time ago God made a choice among you that the Gentiles might hear from my lips the message of the gospel and believe.

⁸ God, who knows the heart, showed that he accepted them by giving the Holy Spirit to them, just as he did to us.

⁹ He did not discriminate between us and them, for he purified their hearts by faith.

¹⁰ Now then, why do you try to test God by putting on the necks of Gentiles a yoke that neither we nor our ancestors have been able to bear?

¹¹ No! We believe it is through the grace of our Lord Jesus that we are saved, just as they are."

Church Membership Denied for Non-Payment of Tithes

It is sad to say that some tithe-collecting pastors have gone to the extent of making "tithing" the standard for assessing church membership. They deny membership to those who do not pay the (Levitical) Tithe. Why does the tithe not include the Charity Tithe (tithe given to widows, orphans, poor and strangers) and the Festival Tithe (tithe for celebrating annual feasts)? Remember that tithing was a part of the Mosaic Law. In the law, when you are guilty of one, you are equally guilty of all, as shown below:

James 2:10-11

¹⁰ For whoever keeps the whole law and yet stumbles at just one point is guilty of breaking all of it.

¹¹ For he who said, "You shall not commit adultery," also said, "You shall not murder." If you do not commit adultery but do commit murder, you have become a lawbreaker.

The Story of a 65-Year-Old Woman

The following is a pathetic story of a 65-year-old Christian:

A 65-year-old wheelchair-bound woman with congestive heart failure was kicked out of her church because she was not paying her tithe, NBC 4 reported. Loretta Davis told NBC 4's Mike Bowersock she was shocked when she received a letter saying she was no more considered a member of her church, The Living Word Tabernacle. Davis made an agreement with the church that she would give 10 percent of her income. Then she became ill and stopped making payments, so the church revoked her membership. "Since Jan. 5, I've been in the hospital 15 times," Davis said. "I've suffered with cellulites since I've had the open heart (surgery)." Davis is no longer paying the church $60 per month from her $592 per month Social Security check, Bowersock reported. "I have my tithes that I was supposed to pay, but I have not paid them since this ha went on," Davis said. "In the time of (Davis's) need, they should be caring, supporting, asking what she needs – help her if she needed help," said Teresa Meeks, who is Davis' daughter. "I was so hurt on what they did to her." The church moved out of its building in Waverly earlier this year and Davis' dismissal has become the talk of the town, Bowersock reported.
In a letter to the editor of the local paper, the former pastor said it is true that Davis lost her membership for not paying her tithes. In the same letter, he said Davis was not kicked out of the church for not paying her tithes. The Rev. Paul McClurg, who started the church, said Davis is still welcome to attend church but is not allowed to be a member. The issue upset Davis' 83-year-old mother so much that she quit the church. [130]

Manipulation #8:

Blessing-Tithing Testimony

Proverbs 14:5

[5] An honest witness does not deceive, but a false witness pours out lies.

One of the schemes through which many have been manipulated to tithe is via Tithing Testimony. It is not uncommon to find on the church podium one or more Christians lining up to testify of what God has done in their lives thanks to their faithfulness in tithing. These Christians try very hard to link any blessings they have gotten so far to the tithes they had given in the past. By attributing divine blessings to their carnal practice of one of the laws, such Christians are simply revealing how deep they have plunged themselves into the spiritual well of *legalism*. Wherever there is legalism, there is pride, and, consequently, condemnation. When you listen carefully to tithe adherents speak about their fidelity in tithing, you can always see the pride on their faces, or hear it from their voices. Performance always breeds pride. However, wherever there is an attachment to grace, there is humility,

---

[130] *Tithing is Not for New Testament Christians!* Internet; accessed 28 December 2017; available from https://tithingstudy.wordpress.com/2011/02/26/the-third-tithe/.

selflessness, calm, dependence, and hope.

Below is a so-called tithing testimony of a Minnesota Christian pediatrician, Nathaniel R. Payne:

> "Regarding my tithing story, I have thought about this for several occasions. I have concluded my whole life has been a testimony on the benefits of paying tithing. I have paid since I was a little boy, as far as I can remember. It is one of the few commandments I can keep with precision. All I have to do is figure out my increase, and the IRS gives me ample excuse to do that. When I was a young man, I received the clear impression that as long as I paid my tithing, I would never be in want of necessities. I have paid my tithing, and I testify I have never wanted for any of life's essentials. It is true there have been many difficult times in my life from a financial standpoint. However, somehow there has always been a way to work through those.
>
> As I contemplate retirement, I have thought much on the financial demands that will be made of me during those years when I am less able to work, or moonlight, or otherwise supplement my income. As I have thought and prayed about this, I have had the recurring feeling and impression that the Lord would honor his promise, and he would take care of my needs. However, it is a matter of faith. It is difficult to exercise faith. Yet it is faith I will need for the future and the present. I know the key to paying tithing is faith, not money. The Lord doesn't care how much tithing we pay, as long as it is a true tithe. Thus, there is no point at which we have enough income to pay our tithing. We pay it as soon as we have income.
>
> I share with you my testimony of this eternal and true principle. The lord honors his promises meticulously. He has promised us the windows of heavens would open, if we would just pay our tithing. I bear testimony this is true.
>
> Nathaniel R. Payne,
>
> Burnsville Stake, Minnesota [131]

4 Motivational Reasons
Why Most Christians Pay Tithes

As a church worker, my interactions with tithe payers have taught me that most tithe payers adhere to the tithing doctrine not simply because they want to be "good Christians." They do so for four main reasons outlined here-below:

(1) To be right with God and the local church.

(2) To invoke God's blessings.

---

[131] Lucy Ekanem, *The Mystery of Tithing: Testimonies of Faith and Sacrifice* (USA: Dorrance Publishing Co., Inc., 2009), 5.

(3) To evade God's curse, which they believe (as they have been consistently taught over the years) is reserved for those who do not tithe, and

(4) To compensate God for any unrighteous habits in their lives.

Point 1 above accounts for one of the motivational reasons for tithing in the United States as reported by Hudnut-Beumier. Below, Hudnut-Beumier tells us that in the United States, many believe they have to give to God through their local church, and they give in order to maintain a good relationship with God.

> At the heart of American religion lies a deep irony. Most religious accounts of why people should support their churches posit a relationship between human beings and a being beyond the human community. The only way to give money to God is to give it to a mediating human institution like a church, or perhaps to engage in direct charity on behalf of God, to provide a dollar or a meal to a beggar because that's what God might do if God were here and worked with the material at hand. Thus religious people pay for God in the sense of paying to be in relation with God through religious institutions they support, and they sometimes pay for God as one might pay for lunch for a friend who is a bit short of money. [132]

This philosophy of "giving to please God" is much more apparent in tithing since, unlike freewill offering, tithing is viewed as fulfilling God's law. And it is a mindset that is not just common to Christians who live in the United States, but can be identified with Christians all over the globe. You can't have your way to "the throne of grace" through the process of "tithing." No, even if you tithe to the least dime. You can only have your way to God's heavenly throne by sacrificing your body to God on a daily basis (Romans 12:1).

Manipulation #9:

Tithing as Personal Revelation

Ezekiel 13:1-3

[1] The word of the LORD came to me:

[2] "Son of man, prophesy against the prophets of Israel who are now prophesying. Say to those who prophesy out of their own imagination: 'Hear the word of the LORD!

[3] This is what the Sovereign LORD says: Woe to the foolish prophets who follow their own spirit and have seen nothing!

Knowing that the collection of tithes is not justified in the New

---

[132] Hudnut-Beumier, *In Pursuit of the Almighty's Dollar*, 7.

Testament Church, some pastors have gone to the extent of telling members of their congregation that God revealed to them personally that their congregation must tithe so as to receive God's financial blessings. And because most of the members want to be rich at all cost, they abide to their pastor's deception. This is very common in Africa-based churches.

And here-below is the word of the Lord concerning those who claim to have seen a vision from the Lord when the Lord has not spoken to them:

Ezekiel 13:9

⁹ My hand will be against the prophets who see false visions and utter lying divinations. They will not belong to the council of my people or be listed in the records of Israel, nor will they enter the land of Israel. Then you will know that I am the Sovereign LORD.

Manipulation #10:

Manipulation from Silence

2 Timothy 4:1-2

¹ In the presence of God and of Christ Jesus, who will judge the living and the dead, and in view of his appearing and his kingdom, I give you this charge:

² Preach the word; be prepared in season and out of season; correct, rebuke and encourage—with great patience and careful instruction.

Another tool of manipulation I have seen displayed by some pastors is that, knowing fully well that tithing is not a Christian doctrine, they have maintained a total silence on the pulpit regarding tithing contrary to the biblical exhortation to preach the truth of the gospel anytime, anywhere. The tithe-collecting pastors know that if they dare to preach an objective message on Tithing as written in the Scripture, their covetousness would be immediately exposed. So, as a route of escape, they maintain an atmosphere of total silence in the pulpit as far as tithing is concerned. This silence enables members of the congregation, who are somehow caught in the middle between the legitimacy of tithing in the church and the fear of attracting a curse for not tithing, to continue to chip in their tithes. The tithe-collecting pastors are cognizant of the fact that an explicit teaching of the biblical tithing practice would cut off the flow of the money. The love of money, they say, is the root of all evil. The love of money made Judas Iscariot to lose his place in the kingdom of God. If these ministers don't change their ways, I'm afraid, the love of money may drive them to the other side, as some have already been driven there as this author writes.

Manipulation #11:

Appreciate-God-for-Grace

2 Kings 5:20-24

[20] Gehazi, the servant of Elisha the man of God, said to himself, "My master was too easy on Naaman, this Aramean, by not accepting from him what he brought. As surely as the LORD lives, I will run after him and get something from him."

[21] So Gehazi hurried after Naaman. When Naaman saw him running toward him, he got down from the chariot to meet him. "Is everything all right?" he asked.

[22] "Everything is all right," Gehazi answered. "My master sent me to say, 'Two young men from the company of the prophets have just come to me from the hill country of Ephraim. Please give them a talent of silver and two sets of clothing.'"

[23] "By all means, take two talents," said Naaman. He urged Gehazi to accept them, and then tied up the two talents of silver in two bags, with two sets of clothing. He gave them to two of his servants, and they carried them ahead of Gehazi.

[24] When Gehazi came to the hill, he took the things from the servants and put them away in the house. He sent the men away and they left.

Appreciate God for His grace is one of the most effective tools of manipulation. It targets not just the non-tithers but particularly the tithers in the congregation. The manipulation goes this way: The believers are told that they have to give a tithe that exceeds the tithe of the Jews as an appreciation to God for bestowing the believers with His unfailing grace. The Jews, who were under the covenant of the Law, did not enjoy this grace. It is, therefore, requisite for the believer to demonstrate by substance their gratitude to God by giving God a tithe that exceeds the minimum ten percent required of the Jews.

The late Billy Graham applied this tool as follows:

> The tithe is the Lord's. If you use it for yourself, you are robbing God. The New Testament goes beyond the Old Testament and teaches that we are to give as God has prospered us. We are to take the tithe as a standard, but to go beyond the tithe as an indication of our gratefulness for God's gifts to us.[133]

Ingratitude to God is sin, said Billy Graham. Graham went further to stress that believers should appreciate God for His grace with a tithe higher than ten percent:

---

[133] Billy Graham, *Are You Robbing God?* Internet; accessed 29 July 2020; available from https://decisionmagazine.com/are-you-robbing-god/.

One of the worst sins that we can commit is that of ingratitude. In the midst of sorrow and trouble, this life has many blessings and enjoyments that have come from the hand of God. Life itself, preservation from the dangers to which life is at every instant exposed, every bit of health that we enjoy, every hour of liberty and free enjoyment, the ability to see, to hear, to speak, to think and to imagine – all this comes from the hand of God. Even our capacity for love is a gift from God. We show our gratitude by giving back to Him a part of that which He has given to us. [134]

Manipulation #12:

Linking Money to Spirituality

2 Corinthians 4:18

[18] So we fix our eyes not on what is seen, but on what is unseen, since what is seen is temporary, but what is unseen is eternal.

The last, but not the least, tool most preachers employ in manipulating their congregation to tithe is by overly raising money to a status it does not occupy in the kingdom of God. They overemphasize the need for money in the church institution. They tell you that the church will soon go bankrupt if you fail to bring your tithes. Quoting Matthew 6:33, they continue, "As the Scripture says, 'Seek ye first the kingdom of God, and his righteousness; and all these things shall be added unto you.' The believer must, therefore, submit their tithes and offerings into the church to support the work of God, and, by so-doing, they will inherit God's spiritual blessings."

Some pastors will even go as far as making the payment of tithes a prerequisite for one's eternal salvation. An exemplary figure to mention here is Pastor E.A. Adeboye, the general overseer of Redeemed Christian Church of God (R.C.C.G.), who, speaking to his congregation, said, "If you do not pay your tithes, you cannot go to heaven. Full stop!" We will comment on this later.

Another preacher who laid emphasis on giving was Billy Graham. Here-below is an excerpt from the late Billy Graham. Like many prosperity preachers, Billy Graham emphasized the need to "give."

"The chief motive of the selfish, unregenerate person is to 'get.' The chief motive of the dedicated Christian should be to 'give.' There are clearly two philosophies about money. The first is Satan's. He says to every man, as he said to Christ, 'All these things I will give you if you will fall down and worship me' (Matthew 4:9). The second philosophy is Christ's. 'Sell all that you have and distribute to the poor, and you will have treasure in heaven; and come, follow me' (Luke 18:22)."[135]

---

[134] Graham, *Are You Robbing God?* Accessed from decisionmagazine.com.
[135] Ibid.

What people do not understand is that when most prosperity preachers tell you to give, they are not saying you should give to the needy in your family or community where charity begins. What they intend by making such an emphasis on giving is that you give the money to them. And when you do, they use the money to acquire the things of their interest, some of which are not even related to the purposes for which the money was given. To ease their conscience and avoid any criticism, they then give a small portion of the money received to a select few as gifts and later have them broadcast in the church newsletter and over the television network.

Glorifying Money

Here-below is another excerpt from Billy Graham where Graham glorifies money (*gold,* as used by him) by associating money with grace, and making it a necessity in the believer's spiritual life.

> "Over and over again, Christ mentioned money. Though His Gospel was spiritual, He had much to say about the material, because there is always a relationship between the two, paradoxical though it may seem.
>
> He said 'Render to Caesar the things that are Caesar's, and to God the things that are God's' (Mark 12:17). So grace and gold are inseparably bound up; and as long as God's kingdom is upon earth, the need of earthly mammon is indicated and is closely tied to our spiritual life. [136]

A Final Word on "Manipulation to Tithe"

2 Peter 3:17-18

[17] Therefore, dear friends, since you have been forewarned, be on your guard so that you may not be carried away by the error of the lawless and fall from your secure position.

[18] But grow in the grace and knowledge of our Lord and Savior Jesus Christ. To him be glory both now and forever! Amen.

One of the main reasons why your pastor has succeeded in manipulating you into giving a tenth of your income is due to your ignorance of the Word of God. As the Scripture above clearly stipulates, the only way through which you can be free from such manipulations is by acquiring the right knowledge. As you have now gained awareness of the manipulative tools used in getting people to tithe, and as you grow in the grace of God by studying God's Word, it will become pretty difficult, if not, impossible, for you to be seduced

---

[136] Graham, *Are You Robbing God?* Accessed from decisionmagazine.com.

by the doctrines and philosophies of men.

Tithing: A Kind of Seed-Faith

1 Timothy 6:8-10

[8] But if we have food and clothing, we will be content with that.

[9] Those who want to get rich fall into temptation and a trap and into many foolish and harmful desires that plunge people into ruin and destruction.

[10] For the love of money is a root of all kinds of evil. Some people, eager for money, have wandered from the faith and pierced themselves with many griefs.

Tithing is analogous to the *seed-faith* doctrine practiced by some Christians today. A person facing a life challenge like barrenness or a chronic disease would be told to sow a seed to God, that is, to give a huge sum of money to God so as to provoke God's intervention in their situation. And this is the same way tithing works. The Christian is told that if they continue to give God their tithes, God will step into their situation and make everything to be in order.

Oral Roberts and the Seed-faith Concept

The concept of seed-faith was fabricated by Oral Roberts (1918-2009), an America-based Pentecostal and United Methodist televangelist. Roberts claimed to have seen a vision in 1977 of a 900-foot Jesus who told him to raise eight million dollars to build a large hospital in Tulsa, Oklahoma. Consequently, Roberts began pressurizing members of his church to give so they could be blessed in return. And millions of people were ensnared by the deceptive words of this preacher. The result was that Oral Roberts became so rich, and the hospital was actually built. However, the hospital stands today as a bankrupt monument, and a testimony to the greediness of a man who enriched himself by hook or by crook.[137]

Tithing, like the seed-faith doctrine, offers false promises of financial blessings to its adherents. It conditions Its adherents to be ever expecting. As a consequence, the tithe-payers keep focusing on what blessings their tithes will generate and never focus on putting to work God's talents in them, which is God's designed method for them to acquire whatever blessings they so desire here on earth.

In seed-faith, as well as in tithing, the gullible are induced to give in

---

[137] Christopher J. E. Johnson, *Tithe Is Not a Christian Requirement*; Internet; accessed 26 July 2020; available from http://www.creationliberty.com/articles/tithe.php.

order to get back, a system that is reminiscent of secular lottery. Seed-faith gives its adherents a false hope that when they give to God $1,000, for example, they will get a hundred fold in return, that is, $100,000. This is what Apostle Paul would describe as *the teaching of demons* (1 Timothy 4:1).

In fact, Oral Roberts happens to be the spiritual father of Bishop David Oyedepo, a Nigeria-based pastor and founder of Winners' Chapel. Prior to travelling over to Japan in 2008 for my undergraduate studies in Theology, I had served as accountant in the central branch of Oyedepo's church in Cameroon (Douala) for close to two years. I witnessed how church members, including myself, were manipulated into paying tithes.

David Oyedepo uses the same tricks as Oral Roberts to lure believers into giving. This is pathetic! To be considered a full member of the church, you must be an active tithe payer. This is just one of the criteria. A record booklet of tithe payers is kept by the church accountant. To determine the extent to which you could be given welfare assistance, the head pastor would have to verify your tithe-payment record with the accounting office.

When the church leadership once realized that not everyone was paying tithes, it threatened to post on the church bulletin the names of all tithe payers. This forced quite a good number of church members into my office who came scrambling to pay their tithes so as to avoid public humiliation. Even though no names were actually published, that method of getting people pay tithes (or whatever form of giving) through persuasion is unbiblical and must be shunned. The kingdom of God doesn't work <u>by force</u>; it works <u>by choice</u>. Tithing in the church can only survive by force, and that's the reason why it cannot be part of the gospel of the good news of Christ. This is one of the reasons why we denounce in this book the practice of tithing in the Church of the new covenant.

Pay Your Tithe or Get Out of Here!

This attitude of linking tithing to church membership is not unique to Winners' Chapel. It has become an epidemic syndrome in a number of church institutions worldwide. In some churches, the situation is worse. Take, for example, the famous American preacher, Ed Young, who boldly said to the congregation in one of his sermons, "Tithe or get out!" [138]

On October 10, 2010, Ed Young went further to make the following utterances:

> "Are you eating the tithe like Adam and Eve did? Are you spending the tithe on a boat or hunting lease? Are you wasting the tithe? ... I've got to ask you (ha ha ha) seriously (ha ha ha). Why are you even coming to church if you're not bringing the tithe? What are you expecting? Just hang out at home, man, play golf. Go somewhere else. You don't need to be here. What are you expecting, man? Are you crazy? You ain't gonna get anything. It's not gonna happen. You're spitting in the wind."[139]

According to this preacher ('preacher' used here for the sake of convenience), the non-payment of tithes is a sin that is equivalent to drug addiction. So, in Young's church, those who do not pay tithes are considered as drug addicts. There is something you may not see beneath Young's statement, which I would like to bring to the surface. Before teachers of falsehood come up with any manipulative statement, they have one agenda in mind: to lure the gullible to subscribe cursorily to their agenda by instilling enormous fear in them.

Analyzing Ed Young's Heretical Statement

Let us now perform a spiritual dissection of Ed Young's statement above, where he equates the Christian who does not pay tithes to a drug addict. Note that eternity in hell is the most dreaded thing to believers, and, I would add, unbelievers. Also note that there is no promise of eternal damnation in hell for defaulters of tithe payment in the old covenant, but there is such a promise of eternal damnation in the new covenant for drug addiction. So, Young knows that linking tithing (an Old Testament law, which no longer applies to New Testament believers) to drug addiction, which leads to eternal damnation, would scare and force the non-tithers in his congregation into submission. That is the trick!

In the same sermon, Young went further to question his congregation why they should even come to church in the first place without bringing the tithe. He then suggested that those without the tithe should have stayed home playing golf. He places 'the money' far above 'the gospel.' He deprives God's people of fellowship simply because of money. Instead of gathering the sheep (Hebrews 10:25) in

---

[138] Internet; accessed on 30 July 2020 from http://youtu.be/ksKon8kunEE; retrieved via http://www.creationliberty.com/articles/tithe.php.

[139] Ibid.

spite of their circumstances, Young scatters them (Jeremiah 23:1) because of their circumstances. Men of such caliber cannot be servants of the kingdom of God but servants of themselves or of some other god. To such men, Prophet Jeremiah would not hesitate to shout, "Woe to you!"

"No Tithe, No Heaven" Heresy

Like Ed Young, Pastor Enoch Adeboye, a Nigerian preacher and overseer of one of the largest church congregations in Nigeria, and, perhaps, in Africa, known as Redeem Christian Church of God (R.C.C.G.), once told his congregation that "Anyone who is not paying his tithes is not going to heaven. Full stop."[140] What Adeboye meant by that statement is that no member of his congregation would gain access into heaven after death if they do not pay tithes. In other words, the payment of tithes is a prerequisite for one's eternal salvation.

By echoing a "Full stop," Adeboye is reiterating the fact that as the general overseer of the R.C.C.G. Church, the statement he had earlier made is final. That is, it is a presidential decree, reminiscent of the papal bull of the Roman Catholic Church in the medieval ages, which cannot be put to question nor altered, not even by the scriptures themselves, but must be followed to the letter. That meeting seemed to have been a pastoral conference. At the end, Adeboye urged the pastors in attendance to take the message to their various local churches, making sure that every church member pays their tithes. You can see the same connection here. The whole game is to force believers into financial submission.

Tithing is a 'works-based' doctrine that the new covenant frowns at. No one "is going to heaven," to use Adeboye's words, because they gave ten percent of their income to God, but those that will "go to heaven" will only make it there because they had embraced, through faith, the gift of grace freely offered by the Lord Jesus Christ. To this last statement, we can boldly say, "Full stop."

---

[140] Internet; accessed 10 May 2020; retrieved from https://www.youtube.com/watch?v=P-0aYfPw1JQ.

10

CONCLUSION

We have seen in the preceding chapters what tithing was really all about. We went further to show how the tithing doctrine was inconsistent with the New Testament Church through an examination of select passages from the New Testament. Lastly, we showed the various tools most preachers employ to manipulate members of their congregation into paying tithes.

Tithing - Not For the Church:

Jesus Knew, The Early Apostles Knew!

When we read the entire New Testament, one fact stands out clearly: Jesus did not preach about tithing, neither did he pay any tithes nor ask his disciples to do so. Paul, a man who wrote almost half of the entire New Testament never in any of his epistles spoke about tithing. The early Church, likewise, never practiced tithing. Was Jesus ignorant of tithing? Were Paul and the early Christians, too, ignorant of the doctrine? No, they weren't. They were so knowledgeable about the truth. These men knew tithing was part of the Law of Moses, and they also knew Jesus had fulfilled the entire Law on the cross (Matthew 5:17). They knew they were no more under the Law of Moses; they were under a new law, the Law of Grace. They knew they could not serve the Law of Moses and the Law of Grace at the same time. They knew that clinging onto tithing meant rejecting grace altogether. They embraced the new, the law of grace, and rejected the old, the law of the flesh otherwise called the Law of Moses.

Therefore, because Christians, who now live under the law of grace, are saved not by the works of the flesh but by grace through faith in the finished work of Christ on the cross, Christians are <u>not required</u> to practice the law of tithing, unlike the Jews, in order to merit divine blessings and eternal salvation.

LOVE is the Answer, not Tithe!

Jesus had summarized all of the laws that are written in the Bible into one: Love God and love your neighbor. This is the commandment that believers of Christ are called upon to adhere to.

Matthew 22:37-40

[37] Jesus replied: "'Love the Lord your God with all your heart and with all your soul and with all your mind.'

[38] This is the first and greatest commandment.

[39] And the second is like it: 'Love your neighbor as yourself.'

[40] All the Law and the Prophets hang on these two commandments."

As it is clearly indicated in the passage above, the only commandment that Christ, the Head of the Church, has given to His Church, the Body, is that the Church should love God and Man. Every other law is hinged on this one. What Jesus is saying is this: "Friends, you don't need to sacrifice burnt offerings on the altar anymore! You don't need to perform ceremonial rites anymore! You don't need to practice tithing to have financial breakthrough or to be saved anymore! All you need is this: Love God; love your neighbor!"

The Three Intentions of "Giving"

And what is Love? Many erroneously give tithes into their local churches thinking such a practice is a demonstration of love toward God. "Giving" is not an exclusive representation of "love." Giving may signify one of three things:

(1) A genuine expression of the feeling of love toward another,

(2) A cover-up of the absence of love toward another, or

(3) A bribe or gesture by the giver to attract favor from the receiver of such bribe or gesture. Such favor may either be the accrual of blessings or the cancellation of the giver's wrongdoings.

Tithing, as a practice of giving a tenth of one's income to God through their local church, falls under the third intention of giving stated above, that is, a bribe given to God to attract God's favor. The reason we say this is because it is a well-established fact that most Christians give tithes into their local churches for two main reasons:

(1) They give out of fear to prevent the curse of God for not tithing, as they have been taught by their pastor. However, the Bible says there is no fear in love (1 John 4:18). If their 'giving to God' comes out of fear of God's curse, it means it is not love toward God.

(2) They give so God can bless them. Their giving is selfish. It seeks their interest, not the interest of God. Such cannot be qualified as a genuine act of love; it is an act of self-centeredness.

Love Is Embracing Christ and His Word

Love is accepting a person or deity as they are, and seeking the good of such person or deity. God Almighty has given all authority here on earth and in heaven to His Son, Jesus Christ (Matthew 11:27). Therefore, anyone who loves God must listen to the Son. Now, the Son is saying, "Behold, I have fulfilled all the laws that held you in captivity. I have nailed them on the cross for your liberty. Now, come unto me all ye that labor and are heavy laden, and I will give you rest. All I am asking you to do is to love my Father in heaven, and to love your neighbor."

Therefore, anyone who practices the law of tithing is walking in flagrant disobedience to the Son of God. Disobeying the Son of God is not an act of love toward God for he who loves the Father loves the Son also and obeys the Son's commands.

Remember, Jesus said:

John 5:23-25

[23] that all may honor the Son just as they honor the Father. Whoever does not honor the Son does not honor the Father, who sent him.

[24] "Very truly I tell you, whoever hears my word and believes him who sent me has eternal life and will not be judged but has crossed over from death to life.

[25] Very truly I tell you, a time is coming and has now come when the dead will hear the voice of the Son of God and those who hear will live.

You will not be condemned if you listen to the words of Jesus and obey them. Only Jesus has the final authority over your life, not tithing or any other religious laws. When you obey His words, you embrace the sacrifice He paid on the cross for your sins. And He is saying to you today, "Love God and love one another."

We believe that having come to the end of this book, you have been charged spiritually. You have come to know the truth about the subject of tithing. With this knowledge, you will begin to experience true freedom in Christ. We kindly ask that you do not keep this knowledge to yourself. Please try to spread it among your friends and neighbours so they, too, can be blessed. God bless.

REFERENCES

Croteau, D. A. (2010). *You Mean I Don't Have to Tithe? A Deconstruction of Tithing and a Reconstruction of Post-Tithe Giving.* USA: McMaster Divinity College Press.

Ekanem, L. (2009). *The Mystery of Tithing: Testimonies of Faith and Sacrifice.* USA: Dorrance Publishing Co., Inc,

Hincks, W. (1830). *The Claims of the Clergy to Tithes and Other Church Revenues.* 2nd Ed. London: Effingham Wilson.

Hudnut-Beumier, J. (2007). *In Pursuit of the Almighty's Dollar: A History of Money and American Protestantism.* USA: University of North Carolina Press.

Kelly, R. E. (2007). *Should the Church Teach Tithing? A Theologian's Conclusions About A Taboo Doctrine.* USA: Writers Club Press.

Wells, A. B. (2007). *The Great Tithing Debate: Condemned If You Do, Condemned If You Don't.* USA: Author House.

Wretlind, D. O. (2006). *Shekels, Dollars, and Sense: A Biblical Theology of Financial Stewardship.* UK: Trafford Publishing.

Online Sources:

Barnes' Notes on the Bible. *Leviticus 27:32*. Internet. Accessed 21 August 2020. Retrieved from www.biblehub.com.

Ellicott's Commentary for English Readers. *Leviticus 27:32*. Internet. Accessed 21 August 2020. Retrieved from www.biblehub.com.

Graham, Billy. *Are You Robbing God?* Internet. accessed 29 July 2020. Retrieved from https://decisionmagazine.com/are-you-robbing-god/.

Johnson, Christopher J. E. (2012). *Tithe is Not a Christian Requirement?* Internet. Accessed 7 September 2020. Retrieved from http://www.creationliberty.com/articles/tithe.php.

Let Us Reason Ministries. *The Origin of Tithing*. Internet. Accessed 28 December 2017. Retrieved from http://www.letusreason.org/doct54.htm.

Sproul, R.C. *Will Man Rob God?* Internet. Accessed 26 July 2020. Retrieved from https://www.ligonier.org/learn/articles/will-man-rob-god/.

Tithingstudy (2011). *Tithing Is Not For New Testament Christians*. Internet. Accessed 28 December 2017. Retrieved from https://tithingstudy.wordpress.com/2011/02/26/the-third-tithe/

YouTube. Internet. Accessed 10 May 2020. Retrieved from https://www.youtube.com/watch?v=P-0aYfPw1JQ.

YouTube. Internet. Accessed 30 July 2020 from http://youtu.be/ksKon8kunEE. Retrieved via http://www.creationliberty.com/articles/tithe.php.

ABOUT THE AUTHOR

Njikang Clovis Mebinaji is a writer, editor, and charismatic teacher of Biblical literature. He was born in Muea, a small town in Cameroon that's located in the outskirts of Buea. In Muea, Mebinaji spent the early years of his life up till when he obtained his undergraduate education. Mebinaji holds two doctorate degrees: one in Theology (2020), the other in Religious Education (2018). He also holds an international master's degree in business administration (2014), a bachelor of Arts in Theological Studies (2012), and a bachelor of Science in Accountancy (2002).

Mebinaji is happily married to Catherine. In February 2020, they were blessed with a baby girl, Mebilyn, their little vibrant angel who at her little age is filled with a great sense of humor toward her parents.